D0090336

GROUP TECHNIQUES
FOR AGING ADULTS

GROUP TECHNIQUES FOR AGING ADULTS
Putting Geriatric Skills Enhancement into Practice

Kathie T. Erwin, Ph.D., L.M.H.C.
National Certified Gerontological Counselor
Largo, Florida

NATIONAL UNIVERSITY
LIBRARY LOS ANGELES

Taylor & Francis
Publishers since 1798

USA	Publishing Office:	Taylor & Francis 1101 Vermont Avenue, N.W., Suite 200 Washington, DC 20005-3521 Tel: (202) 289-2174 Fax: (202) 289-3665
	Distribution Center:	Taylor & Francis 1900 Frost Road, Suite 101 Bristol, PA 19007-1598 Tel: (215) 785-5800 Fax: (215) 785-5515
UK		Taylor & Francis Ltd. 1 Gunpowder Square London, EC4A 3DE Tel: 0171 583 0490 Fax: 0171 583 0581

GROUP TECHNIQUES FOR AGING ADULTS: Putting Geriatric Skills Enhancement into Practice

1 2 3 4 5 6 7 8 9 0 BRBR 9 8 7 6

This book was set in Times Roman by Brushwood Graphics, Inc. The editors were Christine Williams and Kathleen P. Baker. Cover design by Michelle Fleitz. Printing and binding by Braun-Brumfield, Inc.

A CIP catalog record for this book is available from the British Library.
The paper in this publication meets the requirements of the ANSI Standard Z39.48-1984 (Permanence of Paper)

Library of Congress Cataloging-in-Publication Data
Erwin, Kathie T.
Group techniques for aging adults:putting geriatric skills enhancement into practice/by Kathie T. Erwin.
    p. cm.
Includes bibliographical references (p.).

1. Social work with the aged. 2. Social group work. 3. Aged—Care. I. Title.
HV1451.E79   1996
361.6—dc20

96-7905
CIP

ISBN 1-56032-439-2 (case)
ISBN 1-56032-440-6 (paper)

For my most cherished "group,"
my husband Dr. Bert Erwin and our twin daughters, Robin and Kelly.

Contents

Preface

The National Institutes of Health (NIH) issued a consensus statement in 1988 that effectively chastised the mental health profession for failing to strengthen the link between geriatric assessment and follow-up services. Cohen and Geussner's (1989) editorial comment on that NIH statement strongly recommended that gerontologists expand their definitions of assessment to include improved quality of life and other outcomes as well as the mere means to deliver such services. In the years that followed, long-term care facilities came under an increasing weight of regulations that demanded action to show that assessment actually resulted in services for elder patients.

The group program described in this book, Geriatric Skills Enhancement (GSE), shows one answer to the growing concern of how to design elder services that meet the needs identified in geriatric assessments. This book is a practical guide to preparing, arranging, and delivering services to older adults in long-term care, congregate living facilities, or the community.

Who will benefit from this book? Geriatric group leaders, gerontologists, social workers, activity directors, nursing home care-planning teams, geriatric nurse practitioners, adult day-care staff, and students interested in gerontology. The modalities are presented in a format that will be immediately useful to group leaders with varying degrees of clinical skill.

The book is divided into three parts that reflect the theory and design of the group work, specialized modalities, and methods of seeking payment for group work. Part 1, Group Techniques for Aging Populations, introduces the GSE program (Chapter 1) with insight into its theoretical base and designing a group concept for different populations (Chapter 2). The second chapter is packed with practical information for the initial planning decisions, location, obtaining cooperation from staff and families, intake, assessment and a self-quiz on suitability for geriatric group leadership. Some specific planning considerations are given for groups with long-term care residents, cognitively impaired elders (those with Alzheimer's disease and other conditions), elders in adult day-care, and community elders.

Part 2, Geriatric Skills Enhancement Modalities, contains 68 different modalities within 10 themes that comprise the GSE program. In Chapter 3, the classic technique of reminiscence is approached from both simple reminiscence and structured life review. Chapter 4 discusses bibliotherapy—using essays, poetry, mythology, current events, rhymes, and advertisements to engage the four significant stages: receive, perceive, believe, and weave. Chapter 5, "Exploring Values and Roles," is a substantive exercise in "values solidification" that helps elders recapture past strengths for present coping. Values and roles are seen from perspectives of birth order, best friends, families, parenting, work, community service, clichés as imperatives, and personal rules. Sensory awareness (Chapter 6) is a familiar geriatric concept that uses familiar stimuli such as nature, bread making, blowing bubbles, solving a mystery by touch, face mapping, color sensations, pet visits, and a simulated seashore experience. Chapter 7, "Music and Movement," borrows from the effective approaches of music therapy combined with gradual, planned movement. From big band swing music to classics to sing-along favorites, these modalities encourage music appreciation and participation with kitchen band and handbell chorus. Chapter 8, "Phototherapy," uses photo art along with family snapshots and magazine advertisements for a powerful effective group modality. Laughter really is good medicine, as is proved over and again in Chapter 9 with humor groups using tapes of early radio and television comedy shows, essays, clowns, comics, and children's stories. In Chapter 10, spirituality is dealt with not as being about religion, but rather as a larger issue of embracing a belief system for the end of this life and the beginning of what follows. These sensitive group plans include designing rituals of passage and welcome, writing postcards from eternity, defining a spiritual legacy, symbols, mortality, and coping with the death of a group member. Chapter 11, "Art and Expression," offers a kaleidoscope of experiential and discussion options for group members with varying physical abilities from viewing artworks and using art in pain management to creating their own paintings, soft sculpture, collages, and sponge painting. Chapter 12, "Remotivation," takes a combined remotivation and reorientation approach to group introductions, current events, word association, show-and-tell, familiar topic discussions, and a lively beach ball toss cooperative game.

Part 3, Financial Support for Elder Groups, demonstrates how to get paid for geriatric group work through traditional and nontraditional funding sources. Chapter 13, "Managed Payment Systems," deals with the traditional third-party coverages from Medicare, Medicaid, and Medigap. An extensive section on speaking the Medicare language will be highly useful for new service providers. In contrast are the nontraditional payment opportunities revealed in Chapter 14, "Alternative Funding for Elder Groups," including adult day-care, community centers, grants, and nonprofit organizations.

This volume ends with two appendixes, "The GSE Model" and "List of Resources." Both should prove to be valuable tools for the reader.

The best application of this book is as a launching platform for preparing a multimodal geriatric group program in a nursing home, congregate living facility, adult day-care, or community center. The author's objective is that after you read this book you will say with confidence, "I can do that," and then proceed to create an effective group program in your community.

Acknowledgments

I want to thank Elaine Pirrone, Senior Acquisitions Editor, and Bernadette Capelle, Development Editor, for their encouragement and support in preparing this book. A great debt of gratitude goes to all our geriatric group members. A special memory is that of working with the original "D" group. These eight people, ranging in age from 67 to 95, left an indelible mark on my heart and a wealth of ideas that helped to shape the Geriatric Skills Enhancement group programs.

Part One

Group Techniques
for Aging Populations

Chapter 1

Introduction to Geriatric Skills Enhancement

Cast me not off in time of old age, forsake me not when my strength falters.

—Psalm 71:9

"No more 6-week wonders that disappear as fast as they came," the nursing home administrator insisted. "We want a well-rounded program that really meets the needs of our senior population on more than an arts-and-crafts level. Can you do that?" The answer to that question became Geriatric Skills Enhancement, an interactive group program for aging adults.

Geriatric Skills Enhancement (GSE), like the entire field of gerontology, remains an evolving process. The program began by observing patients as they participated in various social and crafts programs conducted by the activity therapists, nurses, or volunteers. What was wanted was for GSE to bridge the gap between the activities or social events and intensive psychotherapy. Observations and patient interviews made it clear that GSE's highest and best role was to work with the skills deficits and psychosocial losses of aging persons at various levels of functioning. Thus, the program components had to be adaptable to differing levels of physical or mental status within the groups. GSE also was to be the kind of program that was easy to integrate within a facility's existing space, schedule, and patient care plans.

In cooperation with the nursing home staff and several geriatric consultants, the types of concerns that are prevalent in limited mobility elder populations such as residents of nursing homes or assisted care homes were identified. A series of informal patient focus groups affirmed the findings of these key issues as

- social isolation and reduced social network,
- decreased income,
- limited mobility,
- declining physical strength and stamina,

3

- frustration with the medical establishment,
- worry or anger about past events, and
- sense of powerlessness over own life.

The Alzheimer's or dementia patients experience those same losses compounded by failing memory, disorientation, and anger or agitation as a response to their condition.
From a study of those key issues came the GSE program mission statement:

> Geriatric Skills Enhancement works to restore the aging adult's sense of worth, socialization, and participation within his or her nursing home or assisted living community. Each program element is planned to stimulate individuals to their highest potential level of functioning, improve mental health outlook, and teach alternative coping skills.

This concise statement of what GSE does, whom it serves, and what it seeks to achieve allows therapists to communicate the essence of the program simply. Brevity in a mission statement is increasingly important because few people have the patience or time to listen to lengthy commentary and theoretical harangues. Another advantage of a concise mission statement is the ease with which GSE's purpose is communicated to patients and their family or guardians.

In addition to the issues derived from the informal patient focus groups, GSE developers met with nursing administrators and treatment teams to hear their comments on matters that needed attention in working with an elderly residential population that, at two facilities, ranged in age from 62 to 98, with an average age of 77. Combining those comments with observations of the patient populations, they formulated a set of working assumptions that predicated their group work.

1 Elders in any level of institutional (noncommunity) residential care can feel compelled to attend a program rather than risk staff disapproval or have to defend their preferences. Knowing this, GSE leaders want to motivate and encourage elders to participate in their groups.

2 Even cognitively intact elders may display short attention spans, tempers, or rapid frustration responses in group. These responses in no way demonstrate the awful lingering myth that "you can't teach an old dog new tricks." Physical pain, mobility problems, or emotional distress are often at the core of these responses. Group leaders have to be aware of these responses and adjust the group pace slightly until a comfortable level is found.

3 Radical changes in elder patient behaviors are frequently related to medications. Leaders must not jump to conclusions about the suitability of a patient for group because of sudden or isolated behavioral changes. The patient may need a hiatus from group during medication changes. Consult with the nursing team and the patient's physician before incorrectly assuming that a patient is no longer suitable for group.

4 Regular attendance at group is not certain even in a residential care facility. A supportive facility will make every effort to have members complete their personal hygiene and be ready for group. However, there are unexpected interruptions in patient schedules due to physician visits, medical appointments outside the facility, and physical illness that account for unexpected absences.

5 A longer length of stay in the facility may result in passive acceptance but does not necessarily imply psychosocial adjustment for the patient.

6 The presence of a large number of patients in the same retirement home does not mean there is a positive climate for socialization. Many patients live together, yet separately.

7 Leaders must demonstrate respect at each contact with every patient, not just those in their groups. They are working in the "neighborhood" where their patients and other patients live and must show their "neighborliness" with words and actions that acknowledge the value and dignity of each patient.

CORE PROGRAM MODULES

The choice of small groups for treatment and the design of those groups is explained further in Chapter 2. The use of groups in elder care is commonplace. However, a substantial number of these gathering events, loosely called *groups,* that occur in the nursing home and assisted care facilities have either minimal or limited psychotherapeutic goals. It's a shotgun blast of activity rather than a laser-focused use of professional resources and patient time. In a review of the current groups at GSE's initial sites, most involved craft making or coffee drinking. The same types of crafts were given to all participants. As a 92-year-old male patient said, "I never messed with doilies and cutouts and I don't want to start now." His comment was echoed by other male residents. Although women generally outnumber men in mixed-gender senior adult care facilities, it is a mistake to assume that all residents are interested in the same activities. Androgyny does not work for older men whose belief systems reject participation in what they consider female-oriented activities as an affront to their gender identity. Younger group leaders are cautioned to park their consciousness-raising agendas at the front door. With this population, respecting gender identities and beliefs about traditional male–female roles is more conducive to developing rapport than challenging or questioning. Gender role beliefs are as sensitive as ethnic and cultural background and constitute significant elements of the self-schema of aging adults.

In reviewing the literature on types of groups for elder patients, a wealth of practical as well as theoretical information on reminiscence, reality orientation, and bibliotherapy was located. Joining these staples in a geriatric group therapy menu is an increasing interest in development and use of art, music, movement, and sensory stimulation. Further citations and discussion of the literature that influenced GSE groups are incorporated in later chapters on program modules. There remains a clear distinction in program design and module scheduling that is as true with geriatric groups as with other groups for other ages. Ingersoll and Silverman (1978) made this elegantly simple distinction in group therapeutic goals: the "here-and-now group" with emphasis on relaxation, communication, and memory training versus the "there-and-then group" using reminiscence, life review, and genograms for self-awareness and acceptance. This dual-track viewpoint is important to GSE's overall goals for enhancing elder self-esteem, socialization, and coping skills in the present by drawing on strengths, talents, and beliefs from the patient's past.

GSE's group schedule began with rotating modules of reminiscence, bibliotherapy, reality orientation and remotivation, and sensory awareness. After several months of getting to know the patients and allowing time for their adjustment to the group process, new modules were added to the rotation, bringing in music and movement, art and expression, phototherapy, humor, spirituality, and exploring values and roles. Early forms of these additional modules were very basic. At times GSE leaders were taking a therapeutic style more often used with younger populations and adapting it to offset the physical, visual, auditory, or memory impairments of an elder population. A share of the credit for the development of new modules belongs to the patients, whose responses, criticisms, and inspired suggestions helped these ideas take shape. The creativity of GSE associates also brought fresh touches to the core concepts.

As you study the GSE core program modules, consider them a travel itinerary that will get you where you want your groups to go. Or you can seek alternative routes with touches that fit your therapeutic style and skills. These modules are also suitable for a "mix-and-match" approach in which you select a set of modules most appropriate for your patients. If any of these modules are currently duplicated in some form within the facility schedule, you may want to work jointly with the activity director or delete that particular module from your program. When it comes to serving the needs of your patients and comfortably working within the overall care system, you want to avoid even the appearance of dueling programs.

STAGES OF GROUP PROGRESSION

Therapists who are trained in group work for adolescents, younger adults, or families often have an excellent background and a totally incorrect mind-set for working with geriatric groups. Although many of the techniques are the same, the measures of effectiveness differ. For example, many therapists and nurses are trained in the group process principles of Corey and Corey (1987) that track four stages in the life of a group: initial, transition, working, and termination. In the best of possible outcomes, these stages flow within a reasonable period of time, leading toward a planned termination date. When the group ends, members can recognize how each has experienced change, learning, socialization, or personal growth. These stages and outcomes are also part of geriatric groups, although with less predictability than with certain other populations or issues.

Beginning Stages of Geriatric Groups

In geriatric groups, more time is often spent in the beginning or initial stage, building rapport with patients and overcoming their resistance to participating in the group. This present generation of senior adults tends to be suspicious and mistrustful of any type of counseling. They were raised on stories of self-sufficiency, with a strong belief in the work ethic backed by social and religious rules of order. From one of those rules came the old saying, "Never air your dirty laundry in public." That belief and others like it are stumbling blocks that elders have to overcome before fully participating in sharing their real selves with the group.

Another faulty attitude to overcome in the beginning stages is why the elder patient was referred to group. Almost without fail, as soon as patients hear that GSE group leaders are psychotherapists and social workers, their eyes open wide with anxiety. Next comes the trembling question, "Does that mean someone thinks I'm crazy?" In the life experience of most senior adults, elective psychotherapy was never an option. Having anything to do with psychology or counseling implied serious personal problems and images of padded cells. It's no wonder that elders view counseling as punishment, abandonment, or spiritual compromise (Erwin, 1993). What we consider sharing feelings and gaining strength from the group experience, many elders see as being dragged to the principal's office and being compelled to answer. Some patients will be hesitant to form attachments within the group as a way of shielding themselves from future losses by rejecting any efforts to bond with others. At times their feelings on this subject sound much like those of a disgruntled adolescent who decides to sever connections with peers rather than face abandonment by them again. Elders nearing their final years of life are also wrestling to balance their world view with their present reality and resolve questions of their spirituality in an affirming rather than a guilt-laden manner.

In forming elder groups, the critical issue is trust. Explaining the purpose of group, how to participate, and rules for confidentiality are important elements, yet they are not enough. In geriatric groups, the therapist is the glue that initially holds it together. The leader must expect to be the primary model of trust, communication, and positive regard. Senior adults were also raised to believe that "actions speak louder than words." Unlike baby boomer adults, elders have minimal experience with support groups or therapy. The closest they have come to groups is often socialization among friends and family members, with the bowling team on weekends, or leading a bridge club. Recreating that atmosphere of friendliness and acceptance is important for this population.

Transition Stage

As the topics or levels of discussion become less superficial, group members in the transition stage are trying to decide whether to connect with others or remain on the sidelines. Some senior adults have already established a pattern of isolation in the crowd, a response that can continue even in a small group. The reason has less to do with the size of the group and more to do with an individual's wall of protection against being emotionally wounded or abandoned. Meanwhile, other senior adults in group will blossom given the opportunity to speak and interact. The group leader can easily identify this transition stage when he or she feels like a dance teacher trying to persuade the reluctant students to stop hugging the walls and participate while not letting the flamboyant students hog the stage.

Some group therapists would label this stage as marked by resistance or defense mechanisms in action. With geriatric groups, a leader has more to gain by promoting safe, slow steps toward risk taking and acceptance than by challenging resistance or defenses. Although those elements may be present, a confrontational approach builds the walls higher with both the person being challenged and those observing. Younger adult groups are more likely to experience power struggles and open conflicts between members. In older adult groups, conflicts are more passive–aggressive in nature.

The transition stage is a major test for the group leader. Members are scrutinizing how effectively the leader handles conflict, motivates without shaming, establishes an atmosphere of trust, and models both tact and acceptance in dealing with group members. Many geriatric groups will spend a longer time in the transition stage than will other types of groups. The leader must avoid showing disappointment or pressing an agenda too rapidly to be beneficial to the group. This is one of those issues in which traditionally trained group therapists are most at risk for failure by trying to follow a timetable that seems to indicate success. Some very effective geriatric groups will vacillate between transition and the next stage, working. To do so is not a mark of failure on the part of the leader or the group. The addition of new members, death of a member, upsets in the physical surroundings, change of therapists, or level of functioning of members are all factors that can prevent rapid or uninterrupted movement through all the expected stages of group progression.

Working Stage

When a group is really working, there is a notably high level of cohesion, trust, and personal safety. Members appropriately assume some leadership roles as they freely, without prompting, interact with others. Confrontation can occur with a positive outcome that is managed by members or the leader. Members are trying new behaviors and encouraging changes seen in each other. The leader begins to enjoy the luxury of releasing some control and responsibility to members. More attention is given to common concerns, progress of change, practicing change in the group, and application of change in environments outside the group.

This description of a working group is a more intense experience than occurs in many geriatric groups. In the latter years of life, individuals are rarely seeking major changes in behavior or beliefs. Rather, they are in need of coping skills, self-esteem, and socialization in an accepting atmosphere. Although fostering these skills constitutes a level of change, the focus is on practicing social skills rather than cathartic or confrontational reactions as a prelude to change. In several types of elder groups, the change in coping is actually a restoration of skills that existed in younger stages of the members' lives. The working geriatric group is frequently a reclamation group aimed at finding positive experiences from the past and ways to apply them to deal with the present.

Cohesion in geriatric groups may range from high to moderate during the working stage. Senior adults relate to this concept as being good neighbors, which in their past experience includes socialization, helping, friendliness, and building relationships outside the family. The leader may have to prompt feedback among group members rather than wait for spontaneous responses. This is a generation that was taught that "If you can't say something nice about someone, don't say anything." For many elders, direct confrontation and questioning the behaviors or ideas of a peer is disrespectful. Don't be surprised if you find a unique group member who is willing to challenge another person's irrational behaviors only to find that member insidiously excluded by the others.

The intensity of the working stage may be difficult to sustain and too arduous for elder members. A suitable adaptation that combines transition and working at a level appropriate to include all group members is a more suitable goal than pushing members to emulate all expectations of a working group.

Closure or Termination Stage

A time-specific group will have a predetermined ending date. All members know the final meeting date and begin to anticipate or dread that date. The leader does not wait until the final session to prepare for termination. This issue is discussed periodically as the group works on a study plan, agenda, or workbook. The closure meeting is a kind of graduation that celebrates each member's progress and allows positive disengagement from the leader and other members. Before leaving, members may be asked to state future goals and receive suggestions for monitoring behavior changes.

Geriatric groups may be time specific, as with a partial hospitalization program, or more open and non–time specific, as part of an institutional program, community outreach, or adult day-care. With the open, non-time-specific groups, there is no single end date for all members. A series of unexpected miniclosures occur at random as a result of the death of a member, hospitalization or illness that interrupts attendance, or transfer of a member to another location. The leader must be prepared to manage these loss experiences, which supersede the current agenda and take one or two sessions to complete. Some facilities make the mistake of trying to ignore the death or disappearance of a senior adult. Fellow residents are not fooled or cajoled into avoiding concern over the mysterious loss. The loss of anyone, particularly a group member, must be processed at the next session. Allowing members a safe place to grieve and talk about how this loss affects feelings about their own mortality is a way that the leader demonstrates respect and genuine regard for each member. Wrapping up this miniclosure with verbal tributes about the departed member can be some of the most cohesive and profound moments that the group will share. From these closure points can emerge new levels of closeness among group members that far exceed anything the leader might attempt to orchestrate.

THERAPIST'S ROLE

The bare minimum qualification for a geriatric group therapist is a solid foundation in group therapy and experience in leading adult groups of various ages. Training in gerontology and geriatric groups is a plus, yet it is not readily available in all areas. A minority of baccalaureate and graduate schools include aging or gerontology within core requirements. Thus, many therapists who desire to work with elders get their training during internships, working with other gerontologists, or learning through continuing education. As the population ages and educators wake up to the underserved needs of senior adults, it is hoped that gerontology will move from being an exotic elective to a more realistic status as an important course in human development and family issues for therapists, social workers, psychologists, and nurses. Until that time, more geriatric group leaders are trained on the job than are taught in classrooms.

As previously mentioned, in the transition and working stages for elder groups, the effective geriatric group leader must temper expectations of progress that were learned about group therapy with younger adults in order to meet reasonable capabilities and needs of a senior adult population. Therapists who have worked with young children sometimes have the best patience and ability to stay tuned to nonverbal clues given by socially isolated and depressed elders.

Geriatric groups are a developing, exciting therapeutic process that holds great promise for the future. All the colleagues who teased me about working in slow motion along with the older population fail to understand that the tempo of geriatric groups places great demands on the leader's energy level and participation. After the third GSE group in a given day, my feeling is more of perpetual motion than slow motion. As the cognitive abilities of group members decline, the involvement of the leader as the motivating force for the group increases. This is not the type of group for leaders who like to quickly reach working stage, then sit back and wait for members to do most of the challenging and accountability for other members. With members at all levels of cognitive functioning, the geriatric group leader can expect to be the spoke of the wheel from which activity begins and through which most action passes.

At the present time, a substantial number of geriatric group leaders in long-term care facilities are social workers and nurses. Other professionals becoming interested in this work include mental health counselors, licensed professional counselors, and psychologists. As of this writing there is no known state licensure for gerontologists. Some practitioners work unlicensed under supervision of a licensed professional or hold a license in one of the categories noted while expanding their training to specialize in gerontology. The National Board of Certified Counselors recognizes the need to demonstrate competence in this field by offering professionals who have earned status as National Certified Counselors the opportunity to qualify as National Certified Gerontological Counselors. Additional professional recognition and specialization standards are needed in various levels to train and identify qualified geriatric practitioners.

Nurse as Group Facilitator

Because psychotherapy is not the focus or approach of every type of geriatric group, it is not imperative in all groups for the leader to be a psychotherapist or psychologist. Nurses have conducted a substantial amount of pioneering work for many years with geriatric groups, within both geropsychiatry programs and nursing homes. An early article (Yalom & Terrazas, 1968) on geriatric group work in a hospital published in the *American Journal of Nursing* was coauthored by a nurse (Terrazas) and a renowned expert on group work (Yalom). Two books that have made an important contribution to geriatric group work are by nurse–author Irene Burnside: *Psychosocial Nursing Care of the Aged* (1973) and *Working with Older Adults: Group Process and Techniques* (Burnside & Schmidt, 1984). Popular nursing journals are a good source of practical recommendations for implementing groups and new ideas on how to work within the theme of an established modality.

In responding to the problems of disorientation, lethargy, and isolation of senior adults in both hospitals and nursing homes, nurses have led the way in defining approaches for reality orientation and remotivation groups. Another modality that hospitals generally refer to as the "nurses' group" is frequently an important educational opportunity in which patients learn about proper medication use, nutrition, sensory stimulation, and how to maintain personal care within the limits of an illness or physical disability.

Nurses with training or experience in psychiatric nursing already have a good background in behavioral interventions, identification of psychosocial deficits, and appropriate responses to depressed or cognitively impaired patients. Other nurses who have work experience in a nursing home or who seek additional continuing education in gerontology can adapt those skills to lead geriatric groups. The best beginning is under the supervision of a psychologist or psychotherapist who is qualified and experienced in geriatric group work and is a willing teacher in group process. This coleader or teaching partnership is most satisfactory when there is no professional snobbery to cloud the relationship. Psychologists and social workers may have more specific education in group work or be given a legal domain under licensure to practice independently as group therapists. However, where it really counts, at the patient's level, nurses have as much potential as psychology practitioners to manage many types of geriatric groups with great skill.

One way I attempt to avoid any semblance of professional hierarchy is to use the term *group leader* for geriatric modalities. Specific cautions are given for group modalities that are psychotherapeutic in nature and more appropriately the domain of psychotherapists or psychologists.

Integration into Treatment Planning

Geriatric group therapy is an increasingly popular and cost-effective means of providing treatment to senior adults. Both Medicare and managed care respond favorably to the use of groups in treatment. The nursing and social services staff in most nursing homes and assisted care facilities are stretched to their limits with physical care and paperwork. Such a workload makes individual counseling on a regular basis almost impossible. Through group modalities, there is the potential for more patients to receive treatment on a regular basis.

The group leader's chart notes and summary of the group process (presented in chapter 2) give useful input for the treatment team. When possible or at least at an annual review, the group leader needs to be included in the treatment team planning session for each patient involved in group. GSE group leaders also need to conduct their own quarterly discussion of each group member's participation in and suitability for group. Looking at each patient in the total picture as well as in the limited view seen in the group is necessary for group leaders. Group work does not operate independently of any other treatment or activities that members engage in during other periods of the day. The ideal result is for some positive effects of group work to spill over into a patient's other interactions with residents or staff. Regular communication between the group leader and the treatment team enhances the work of all as well as the potential for good results with mutual patients.

Chapter 2

Designing a Group Concept
for Different Populations

One ought, every day at least, to hear a little song, read a good poem, see a fine picture, and, if it were possible, to speak a few reasonable words.

—Johann Wolfgang von Goethe

Goethe's recommendation is an excellent foundation for a geriatric group program: a combination of music, reading, fine arts, and discussion. Gerontologists know that the only commonality among patients is that of aging. Otherwise, the needs of aging adults are as varied as those of young adults or adolescents. Along with varied needs is the consideration of differing physical and cognitive abilities. There is no one-size-fits-all geriatric group. Rather, the trend is toward the integrated or metatheoretical approach favored by GSE as offering more flexibility for practical application in the field (C. I. Cohen, 1990; Leszcz, 1990; Moberg & Lazarus, 1990). *Metatheoretical* is used here to mean a planned and purposeful eclecticism rather than a sloppy excuse for lack of any theory or concept.

An important inspiration in GSE's program development comes from the multimodal therapy of Arnold Lazarus. Using his BASIC ID (behavior, affect, sensation, imagery, cognition, interpersonal relationships, and drugs; Lazarus, 1976) in evaluating elders for group gives the most complete and useful procedure for intake, group assignment, and monitoring. This acronym serves as a reminder to assess patients for these factors. The BASIC ID is used for pregroup intake; the results affirm the need for a multimodality interactive approach. GSE's model makes one addition, making it the BASIC IDS, with the S representing the spiritual dimension. Further explanations in Chapter 10 demonstrate the significance of spirituality in resolving important questions and making satisfying connections that are concerns for persons reaching the latter stage of life.

A PREVIEW

What follows in this chapter is a wealth of information on how to begin a GSE-style geriatric group program. The intent is that you will be spared some of the on-job-training experiences that accompany program development. Leaders and therapists who have experience in implementing group programs are probably already deep into the modality chapters. This is no place to tune out. Much of what you learn here has a direct relationship to how to get paid for your work. Part 3 gives more information on dealing with third-party payers, finding sponsorship for group work, and completing the necessary paperwork for payment.

INITIAL PLANNING DECISIONS

Several issues need to be resolved by the group leaders or the treatment team during the planning stages of a geriatric group regardless of functioning level. Don't go any further until you answer these 10 basic questions:

1   Will this be one module within a program or a stand-alone group?
2   What is the age range of the group member population?
3   Will this be a mixed-gender or gender-segregated group?
4   Are group members of comparable mental status? Combining cognitively intact, cognitively impaired, and psychotic members in the same group is complicated and of questionable therapeutic value.
5   Are additional staff required to safely transport members to group?
6   Does the group activity require writing, reading, movement, or hearing?
7   What adjustments can be made for members with physical impairments?
8   Will this group be open or closed and for what length of time?
9   What are the overall treatment goals for this group?
10 What level of skills and experience are required for the group leader(s)?

LOCATION

As real estate specialists know, the key to successful property development is "location, location, location." That's also true for geriatric group programs. Like many other programs, GSE works within existing long-term care facilities. Location of your group room and amenities are very important. In the early stages of presenting your program to a facility, carefully survey potential group locations. GSE was given reserved use of a community room near the main unit with ample space for chairs and wheelchairs. This spacious room had windows and a piano, and the doors could be closed for group privacy. Indeed, this location served our adjustment and depression groups well. Much to the leaders' dismay, this wonderful location proved to be a nightmare when working with cognitively impaired groups. Although most of these group members were ambulatory, they were highly resistant to leaving the familiar surroundings of their units. Many of these patients were at high risk for wandering, which sent the leaders on a few unplanned sprints in pursuit. Although the leaders enjoyed working in this spacious room, it proved totally disastrous for cognitively impaired groups.

What worked with the confused elder groups was to remain in a smaller, yet more secure, living room area of each unit. Occasionally, nongroup members watched at the door or wandered inside. Our group members wandered outside and back again. To the leaders' surprise, there was far less wandering, disruption, and inattention during groups held on the restricted access units than in the larger, distant room. The point of sharing this discovery is to remind leaders to be flexible. During remodeling of a unit, group was held by making a circle of chairs at the end of a hallway. To the leaders' amazement, this unseeming location still worked better for confused elders than moving them to the adjacent Alzheimer's unit with an identical floor plan. Certainly having a choice of several possibilities within a facility improves the odds. Regardless of how much the leader likes a group location, what matters is how well it works for the group.

STAFF COOPERATION

Even if your geriatric group is a totally self-contained program with its own leaders and materials, you are not an island within the facility. Attitudes of nursing and patient care staff can make or break your group program. If possible, before making that final commitment attend a staff meeting and present a brief overview of your geriatric group program. Watch the faces. The looks of disdain GSE leaders received were not in opposition to the concept but rather were a nonverbal groan over still another schedule to meet in an already busy daily care agenda. These are the people on whom you depend to get your group members dressed, fed, and ready for transport. Without their cooperation, your program will fail miserably.

GSE begins its relationship with facility staff by presenting in-service training on topics of mutual interest such as communicating with cognitively impaired elders, dealing with caregiver burnout, and the role of groups in reducing social isolation for elders. What seemed obvious to leaders, yet remarkable to the staff, is that leaders did not behave like the experts coming in to overwhelm and issue orders. The leaders said that they wanted to be part of the treatment team, and their actions with the staff affirmed those words. The leaders also participated frequently in treatment team meetings and remained available by phone or appointment to visiting family and primary care physicians.

Meet periodically with the facility's social services or activity director to discuss future scheduling. A few times during the year, particularly Christmas holidays, there were unusual demands on space and time. Knowing in advance about these interruptions from the norm helped to avoid conflicts. Also, leaders need to impress on social services and nursing staff the importance of regular group attendance. This is not the optional drop-in-and-hear-the-local-scout-group-sing event. As staff begins to appreciate the therapeutic benefit of regular group participation, they will make the extra effort to arrange outside medical and dental appointments at times that do not conflict with the group schedule.

In short, GSE leaders gave cooperation and respect to the facility staff and received the same in return. As a result of establishing a professional relationship with positive regard given to all, from the administrator to the aides, leaders experienced minimal problems with having patients ready and available for group.

FAMILY COOPERATION

A comparable personal contact approach is valuable in persuading family, legal guardians, or trustees to allow enrollment of their elder or patient in the group program. Most of your potential group members, even those who are cognitively intact, depend on another party (family or professional) to make medical and financial decisions.

The easiest way to present the group program is at an invited family–guardian–trustee meeting. Many facilities have regular family support groups that are excellent vehicles for explaining and updating progress of your program. If not, ask permission to send invitations for a special family group meeting held at the facility. Provide refreshments and keep the agenda brief, with ample time for questions.

Prepare an introductory letter containing the essential information you shared with the group and send it to any families, guardians, or trustees who were unable to attend the meeting. Don't just mail the necessary enrollment paperwork presented in Part 3. That's too impersonal. Write a letter in a conversational tone or make a cassette tape of opening remarks about the geriatric group program and how it serves patients' needs.

Remain in contact with representatives of enrolled patients and potential patients. Your group can mail a quarterly letter with updates on group projects. Better still, offer to write a general update for the facility newsletter. This worked great for GSE and gave it a monthly forum for reporting on and creating interest in its programs. The column gave a paragraph summary on the activities and special events for each group. Any time that GSE leaders made presentations to professional therapist associations or published writings, this was shared in the column. Several times families of new residents read about the groups and inquired about enrollment before leaders even received the nursing director's request to evaluate the new patients.

A detailed summary was prepared annually for each patient and sent to his or her representative. These were written in nonclinical, easy-to-read terminology. Comments and observations about the patient from every GSE leader who worked with that patient were included. The report closed with treatment recommendations and goals. GSE leaders announced in the facility newsletter when to expect the next report. These simple techniques saved telephone or meeting time and promoted good communication. Whatever methods you choose, find ways to communicate regularly with family, guardians, or trustees.

ARE YOU RIGHT FOR THIS WORK?

Group work with elders requires more direction, encouragement, empathy, psychological support, and leader interaction than with other adult groups (Burnside, 1973). As previously mentioned, leaders come from many therapeutic and health care backgrounds. A degree in gerontology is not guarantee of success as a geriatric group leader. Other characteristics and abilities are a greater predictor of success and satisfaction in working with aging adults. The most effective GSE leaders are (a) genuinely interested working with elders; (b) believe that elders have a right to pleasure, socialization, personal growth, and unconditional respect regardless of age, physical limitations, or cognitive impairments; (c) enjoy being creative and flexible in conducting groups; (d) willing to seek continuing education and training to further skills in geriatric group work and therapeutic issues of aging; and (e) excited about the potential for program development and contributing to the growing body of knowledge about group work with elders.

The program director needs to regularly monitor these qualities by observing leaders in action during group. Another important need is for periodic meetings with leaders to discuss both their work and how they feel about their work. Leaders are not immune to grief and loss reactions that are more frequent in working with elder groups than with many other populations. Leaders must continually adjust their expectations, renew their enthusiasm, and celebrate their efforts.

GLEANING THE MOST
FROM GSE GROUP SUMMARIES

Each chapter on group modalities explains how to conduct groups within that framework. Think of this as a menu with potential variations that are only as limited as the group leader's creativity. To become familiar with the structure of this summary, the sample below explains the format for presenting each group.

   1 *Title*—A title or theme for every group program is helpful for directing the attention of the group and the group leader toward the activity. Smart group leaders will write brief abstracts (25–50 words) on each theme. These abstracts are attachments or references that may substitute for rewriting this information on dozens of patient charts each day. Most facilities appreciate the paperwork reduction in their charts as much as group leaders do.

   2 *Goals*—If you never identify the target, there is no consistent way to aim and hit it. Group leaders must avoid the trite assumption that just being in group is a benefit, therefore surely some goal must have been attained. Wrong! Leaders are responsible for defining goals for the group and for each member. Individual goals may be among those determined by the treatment team. Those goals may be augmented by in-group goals set for each member articulated by the group leader with as much member involvement as possible. To simplify this presentation, *goals* refers to *group goals.*

   3 *Process*—How do we get there from here? Process is the therapeutic superhighway to personal growth and change. Within groups, the leader may have to alter or expand the process in response to the members. However, effective planning requires selecting a process that is suitable to the members' functioning and achievement of group goals. Don't get stuck on the off-ramp of indecision.

   4 *Outcomes*—The frequent admonition "Be careful what you ask for, because when you get it, you'll have to deal with it" is excellent advice for group leaders. For example, reviving memories and past events is not always a tranquil trip down nostalgia lane. What will you do if the memories are painful, traumatic, or obsessive? Do you deal with this problem in group or out of group? Is the theme or process likely to produce a negative outcome? What is the therapeutic usefulness of this with your elder group members? Is there a way to explore the same material yet guide the process toward positives? Here's where the group leaders' planning or consultation needs to include anticipation of positive or negative outcome before proceeding. Other outcome measures (as requested by third-party payers) are slanted more toward the cause–effect relationship of group work with patient improvement or maintenance. Group leaders need more than anecdotal evidence of change to satisfy these inquiries. Establishing a scale or rating method is important, as is applying it consistently.

5 *Equipment list*—As theaters use scenery and TV commercials display how to use products, you'll discover endless ideas for using common items, photos, and other items to support group modalities. This section suggests purchased and assemble-it-yourself items for use in group. Many of the visual aids or memorabilia recommended for different group themes are common household items. Supplies for art and writing projects can be purchased inexpensively from the school supply section of general merchandise stores or discount office supply companies. A favorite all-purpose item is referred to as a *marker board*. This is a white, slick-surfaced board with an aluminum or wood frame that can be affixed to the wall (with permission of the facility) or rested on an easel. Using special colored markers and an eraser, the write-on board is easy to use and clean. Because it does not use chalk like schoolroom blackboards, there is no chalk dust to irritate sensitive persons. These write-on boards come in several sizes and price ranges. Another device that greatly assists communication with hearing impaired or visually limited persons is the popular child's toy Magna Doodle, made by Tyco. Using the attached magnetic drawing pen, the group leader writes or draws a bold imprint on the broad, white face. The sliding eraser at the bottom clears the image with a swift motion so that the communication flows at a natural pace. Several hearing and visually impaired persons were able to participate in group after the leaders began using this simple toy. Purchase the full-size (not the travel-size) Magna Doodle at toy stores or discount department stores.

ASSESSMENT AND INTAKE

The presence of an elder in a nursing home or community program is not sufficient evidence of suitability for group. Watching some poorly constituted groups in other facilities leads one to wonder if availability was the only qualification assessed. Group gurus Corey and Corey (1987) emphasized the importance of pregroup screening in a private session with the leader.

An advantage of working in long-term care facilities is that there is more documentation on each patient that can be reviewed by the leader before the assessment. A high-quality facility does an excellent job of preparing each patient's social history, diagnostic workups, staff observations, and treatment team recommendations. Obtaining permission to use this information as part of the group intake process also saves time and duplication of effort. If you provide groups within a community elder program or adult day-care, you can expect to find less background information. The less available intake information, the more time (often unpaid) you will spend.

GSE's basic assessment package for all groups includes the Folstein Mini-Mental State Exam, the Geriatric Depression Scale, and the Life Satisfaction Index. The Mini-Mental State Exam (Folstein, Folstein, & McHugh, 1975) is an easy-to-administer, nonthreatening way to determine level of cognitive functioning. As an indicator of mood, GSE leaders obtained more completed interviews and better information from the Geriatric Depression Scale (Brink et al., 1982, 1985; Parmalee, Katz, & Lawton, 1989; Yesavage et al., 1983) with its yes and no responses than from the frequently used Beck Depression Inventory. A study by Parmalee and Katz (1990) found the Geriatric Depression Scale to be as reliable and valid for measuring depressive symptoms in Alzheimer's and cognitively impaired elders as with cognitively intact elders in long-term care. The Life Satisfaction Index (Neugarten, Havighurst, & Tobin, 1961) is a long-standing measure of well-being in older adults that focuses on zest for living, congruence, self-esteem, and mood. Over the years, this index has been dissected by psychological researchers and criticized by some (Abraham, 1992), and others have attempted to replace it with, for example, the Salamon–Conte Life Satisfaction in the Elderly (Salamon & Conte, 1984) and Memorial University of Newfoundland Scale of Happiness (Kozma & Stones, 1980). To this point, the Life Satisfaction Index has adequately served GSE leaders' purposes in learning more about the patient's feelings about self and life status. Although the questions require only an agree–disagree response, the leaders have found that the questions often lead to further disclosures by the patient that are extremely useful in the assessment.

With day-care and community elders for whom minimal, if any, diagnostic impressions or social histories are available, add the Direct Assessment of Functional Status (DAFS) or Structured Assessment of Independent Living Skills to the intake assessment. Both instruments give a broader picture of an elder's ability to perform activities of daily living as well as of his or her psychosocial and cognitive skills.

This author was privileged to observe Dr. David Lowenstein as he conducted DAFS interviews at the Wein Center for Alzheimer's Disease and Memory Disorders in Miami Beach, Florida. His calm, reassuring, conversational manner communicated a sense of genuine interest that connected with the confused, agitated elders and resulted in completed interviews. After observing several other geriatric assessment professionals with more terse and distant styles, Dr. Lowenstein's approach validated the author's belief that the patient is more important than the process. GSE intake and assessment is more than a clinical evaluation, it is an opportunity for the active listening, learning about potential group members, and demonstrating positive regard that is the foundation for trust. So put your lab coats in the laundry, dress casually, push away from your desk, and do whatever is possible to make the assessment a comfortable experience for the elder interviewee.

Planning Groups for Long-Term Care Residents

The National Institutes of Health (NIH; 1991) estimated that 15–25% of nursing home residents have symptoms of major or minor depression. That is not surprising if you consider the losses, illnesses, and significant life changes that typically precede entry to a nursing home for an indefinite period. The NIH study further found high rates of new depression cases: that within a year 13% of long-term care residents experience new depressive episodes, and 18% manifest new depressive symptoms. Clearly, this is more than an initial adjustment reaction. Depression, sadness, hopelessness, helplessness, loneliness, and repressed resentment are more common than walkers in most nursing homes, regardless of the quality of physical care or attractiveness of the environment.

In assessing cognitively intact nursing home residents for GSE groups, use the intake interview as an opportunity to develop rapport between the interviewer and the resident. Often in responding to a question, the resident elaborates by expressing feelings or concerns that give pertinent clues for individual treatment goals. The most common treatment goals for this segment of the nursing home population are reducing social isolation, increasing verbal communication, demonstrating a reduction in depressive symptoms, and improving self-esteem. The predominant concerns observed during intake are likely to be included in the resident's treatment plan for psychosocial goals defined by the treatment team. Be specific in determining how to observe and measure progress toward goals. For example, reducing social isolation may be demonstrated in several ways: choosing to attend group at least two or three times weekly, greeting other members without prompting, or agreeing to work with another member outside group to prepare for the next session. When observing growth and change, do more than chart the observation. Take time outside of group to compliment the elder's efforts and encourage continued participation.

The full range of GSE modalities can be used with this population. In fact, elders tend to appreciate the variety and are more interested in regular attendance when themes rotate than with a long series of one theme. After several combinations of single-session and extended themes, GSE groups for this population frequently offered one weekly group that continued for several sessions on a single theme (i.e., life review or art project) while rotating themes for the other weekly sessions. During busy holiday periods or times when new members were entering group, the group returned to single-session themes and lighter topics.

Planning Groups for Cognitively Impaired Elders

GSE's cognitively impaired elders resided in dementia-specific care units within a long-term care facility. Because of the short attention spans and wandering behaviors typical of this population, assessment can be an adventure. First, have a nurse or staff person who relates well to the elders introduce you casually and draw you into the conversation. Next, allow elders to choose the interview location. They may feel safer in their rooms or in the community area. Make every effort to avoid taking confused elders away from their safety zone and into a typical closed testing office. Such an experience is needlessly traumatic for both elders and interviewer. Finally, keep it short. A better result may be obtained by conducting an hour's worth of intake in two half-hour sessions. Good results can also be achieved by completing intake interviews while walking with a resident. Once mastering the art of clipboard notetaking, do intakes and power walking simultaneously.

Some themes from every GSE modality are suitable for cognitively impaired elders. The critical factor in making plans for these groups is to coordinate modalities with group members' levels of functioning and expressed interests. Lindeman, Downing, Corby, and Sanborn (1991) recommended that group activities be designed to minimize cognitive deficits and enhance present skills of the participants. Including at least one remotivation group weekly and rotating with other themes is effective. All GSE groups with this population spent at least the opening minutes with an introduction and a brief reality orientation exercise before introducing the modality for the session. Bring along at least one activity that is enjoyed by the group as a backup. Then if the group quickly loses interest in the primary modality, you can finish the session on a positive note. GSE's lower functioning groups rallied to a sing-along of old favorites from the 1930s and 1940s. Occasionally after just a few songs to change the pace, they were ready to return to the planned activity for the group. Other times, the leader had to be creative and flexible enough to respond to the group's unspoken messages of boredom, frustration, and restlessness.

Planning Groups for Adult Day-Care and Community Elders

Community-dwelling elders have psychosocial needs similar to those of cognitively intact elders in residential care. Only here, leaders work without the advantage of social history, diagnostic background, and staff observational information to supplement their assessments. Remain aware of social research and community issues of significance to the elder population. For example, depressive symptoms are present in 15% of community residents over age 65, and the instance of suicide among depressed elders is higher than for the general population. On a local level, elders face greater age discrimination or social barriers in some communities. Whatever affects their emotional state is a potential group issue. Leaders who are aware of these topics can effectively integrate them into a modality. These groups may be the only forum in which an elder feels comfortable sharing an opinion without criticism.

Adult day-care populations may be more stratified by cognitive functioning than are community programs. On the basis of the other elements of the adult day-care program and the participants' needs, you may be contracted for specific types of groups such as remotivation or bibliotherapy. If so, begin there until you determine other modalities that might be effective for each group. After establishing groups and demonstrating professionalism to the staff, the leader has a more sound basis on which to propose alternative modalities.

Community elders are usually more mobile and self-directed. For them, a group program must be attractive, accessible, and authentic. Piquing their curiosity about the themes and emphasizing the socialization of group are attractive. An accessible location for groups needs to be centralized with nearby parking and wheelchair accommodations, easy to find, and downstairs or with a reliable elevator. To be authentic, groups must provide a realistic opportunity for all participants to learn, interact, and enhance their well-being.

Because community elders retain strong connections to their family, friends, and neighbors, it is important to know more about the cultural identity of minority group members. Never assume that an elder who has lived in the same city for most or all of his or her life is fully assimilated into the predominant culture. Strong familial ties and a love of the birth heritage continue throughout life regardless of the country in which the elder lives. Appreciating this diversity within groups is important for all members to feel valued and willing to participate. The multicultural group also has a golden opportunity to learn and grow by sharing their heritages.

A group leader needs to understand and accept the cultural differences between himself or herself and the minority group members. Typical American thinking emphasizes mastery over self and environment while American Indians and Asian Americans are satisfied to be in harmony with others and nature. Although important for all elders, respect is key to developing rapport with African Americans, Asian Americans, and Hispanics. A very basic demonstration of respect is addressing all group members as Mr., Mrs., or Ms. unless they grant permission to use first names. African American elders recall life under segregation where there was a broad distrust of Whites in authority, which may carry over initially to feelings about a White group leader. Extended family and internal family hierarchy is so strong with Hispanics and Asian Americans that their elders may seem reluctant to talk about feelings and concerns to persons outside the family (Sue & Sue, 1990). Leaders are advised to learn about the multicultural heritage of group members both from studying and from sincere conversations with minority elders.

Turning a Smorgasbord into a Feast

Before stuffing your brain with ideas on the GSE modalities to the point of information indigestion, take a break. This program was developed and refined over several years. Rather than being like a smorgasbord with too much to fit on one plate, GSE group modalities are like well-prepared courses for a royal feast. When served properly, each modality satisfies a particular hunger and prepares the emotional palate for another stimulating experience.

In planning geriatric groups, begin with variations on themes or approaches that are familiar. Then gradually sample and develop to taste. In time, add your style to the groups as much as a fine chef does in preparing a gourmet feast. Bon appetit!

Part Two

Geriatric Skills Enhancement Modalities

Chapter 3

Reminiscence

I cannot but remember such things were, that were most precious to me.

—William Shakespeare, *Macbeth*

Memories are the subject of endless songs, poems, and stories. How often do you hear people of all ages say, "I'll never forget the time . . . "? Sharing memories is sharing an important part of yourself and your experiences. Much therapeutic emphasis in working with survivors of traumatic events is in recovering memories to resolve the distress. Equally strong is the opposing viewpoint claiming that therapists are planting false memories or improperly interpreting true memories. Setting aside this volatile issue, it does affirm the potentially life-changing impact of memories.

PRACTICAL VALUE

In working with elders as therapists, nurses, or family caregivers, one can tune out each time Grandma tells the same story again or use that memory to help her deal better with present circumstances. This approach is known as reminiscence, which can be engaged in group or individual work with senior adults. Reminiscence is a widely accepted technique for using an elder's natural desire to talk about "the good old days" as a means of recalling past strengths and contentment to enhance coping in the present. Sadly, the repetition of or even obsession with certain stories from the past is frequently met by caregivers with frustration, anger at what is incorrectly perceived as losing touch with the present, or dismissiveness of the value of what can be learned from those memories. Group leaders must refrain from such destructive responses. As geriatric group members participate in reminiscence, they discover that who they were is a vital part of who they are today.

Remembering past events can be as comforting to senior adults as warm cocoa on a chilly winter morning. The positive feelings that memories can evoke are now the subject of an entire magazine, *Reminisce*, that is filled with stories, photos, humor, and homespun advice. Its readers are the authors of material featured in this publication. Consider how many untapped reminiscences lay waiting for discovery in your geriatric groups. If you have conducted reminiscence groups, you know what it is like to be amazed at the wealth of experiences and living history represented by group members.

REMINISCENCE IN THE LITERATURE

In the therapeutic literature, reminiscence is frequently subdivided into simple reminiscence and life review. Butler's (1963) groundbreaking article on life review laid the foundation for the value of reminiscence with a life-review focus. Butler challenged the mind-set of health professionals who were quick to dismiss senior adult reminiscences as a sign of their losing their faculties rather than of their engaging in an adaptive process of aging. Later articles by Kaminsky (1984), Birren (1987), and Tobin and Gustafson (1987) supported Butler's belief about the benefits of reminiscence.

LoGerfo (1980–81) described three distinct types of reminiscence: informative, evaluative, and obsessive. The evaluative type is most like Butler's (1963) life review. Informative reminiscence is the timeless tradition of sharing stories and passing along family traditions. Obsessive reminiscence is rumination linked with guilt, fear, mourning, or self-deprecating beliefs that need resolution more than repetition. Inexperienced group leaders are known to allow these pity parties of obsessive reminiscence to damper the group's effectiveness and fail to address the real needs of the distraught participants.

Sherman and Havinghurst (1970) suggested that an increased desire to recall memories correlates with aging. Acting on this desire enhances adjustment, self-acceptance, and ego strength according to Havinghurst and Glasser (1972) and C. N. Lewis (1970). M. Lewis and Butler (1974) showed how memories can have psychotherapeutic impact in improving self-worth and perspective by reliving past events through the eyes of others. Rather than use further space to detail the many early articles on reminiscence and life review, readers are referred to Watt and Wong (1991), who prepared an excellent taxonomy on this subject that is particularly suitable for students, researchers, and group leaders in training.

NEW APPROACHES TO REMINISCENCE

More recent articles that were useful in formation of GSE's reminiscence module expand on areas or new applications of this technique. Lowenthal and Marrazzo (1990) developed "milestoning" to recapture positive memories that can balance present distressing circumstances or being stuck in negative memories. Milestoning does not aim at the full spectrum of positive and negative experiences as does traditional life review. Thus, the milestoning approach is more in harmony with the GSE's primary use of reminiscence to recall past strengths and contentment as means to enhance coping in the present. Wallace (1992) placed a positive emphasis on life review by using narrative interviews. GSE group leaders used a similar technique during one ongoing module that is presented later in this chapter. The positive slant to life review sidesteps traumatic events and steers away from obsessive reminiscences. With this slant, groups can be facilitated by a variety of health professionals, including supervised interns or students coleading with a professional. More intense life-review techniques can evoke abreactions and catharsis are that best managed by experienced professionals. Selecting a group leader for life review demands serious consideration and consultation with a psychiatrist, psychologist, or other appropriately licensed and qualified professional.

CATEGORIES OF REMINISCENCE

Both life review and basic reminiscence have branched out into a variety of subcategories within the overall concept. Although the debate remains as to whether life review and reminiscence are essentially the same or significantly different, there is no consensus. This author agrees with Merriam (1989) that these techniques, although similar, are qualitatively and structurally different. Webster and Haight (1995) supported this distinction by defining reminiscence as highly spontaneous, with little structure as compared with life review, which is more structured and comprehensive. The following is a taste of the smorgasbord of possibilities for therapeutic use.

Life Review

Authors	Approach
Meyerhoff and Tufte (1975)	Weekly life review classes
Koch (1977)	Poetry and expressive arts
Edinberg (1985)	Music, scents, images, and items
Hately (1985)	Spiritual themes in life history
Birren (1987)	Guided autobiography in group
Sweeney (1990)	Early recollections within an Adlerian context
Crose (1990)	Gestalt techniques
Waters and Goodman (1990)	Guided imagery life-review autobiographies
	Systematic interviews

With reminiscence becoming more distinct in its approach, specific techniques acknowledge the need to deal with different types of memories. LoGerfo (1980–81) made this concept clear when she differentiated among three ways to engage in reminiscence. Informative reminiscence is a pleasurable recall of favorite stories of people, places, and events that can be used to rebuild self-esteem. Evaluative reminiscence most closely resembles life review. A more structured personal history, evaluative reminiscence explores an individual's strengths and weaknesses to achieve resolution of the past and self-acceptance. Obsessive reminiscence can be prolonged grief, dissociating from the present by choosing to retreat into the past, and generally getting stuck in a counterproductive activity. Informative and evaluative approaches can be effective and used in many ways. Obsessive reminiscence requires redirection and a safe place to release negative emotions that are more appropriate for a grief and loss group or individual therapy. Such intense release of emotional pain needed for healing is rarely desirable in aging adult groups. Here are some ideas that preceded or expanded on LoGerfo's concept.

Reminiscence

Authors	Types of reminiscence
Kaminsky (1975)	Dreams, images, and songwriting
Kaminsky (1984)	Living history drama
Clements (1982)	Recreational reminiscence
Merriam (1989)	Simple reminiscence
Watt and Wong (1991)	Escapist reminiscence
	Instrumental reminiscence
	Integrative reminiscence
	Narrative reminiscence
	Obsessive reminiscence
	Transmissive reminiscence
Erwin (1992)	Casual—stories or free association
	Relational—important relationships
	Analytical—life review
	Defensive—uses defense mechanisms
	Obsessive—rumination
Creanza and McWhirter (1994)	Life themes and gender issues
Meacham (1995)	First standpoint—accurate recall
	Second standpoint—discover meaning
	Third standpoint—social construct

INTERACTIVE METHODS AND GROUP ACTIVITIES

So many group workbooks speak in generalized terms that advise the leader to "set the mood," "find a common theme," or "integrate feelings with memories." That's more therapy-speak. What does that really tell you about how to plan and run geriatric groups? Not much. In this and every group module chapter, a series of actual group activities is outlined for you.

Leaders can use the suggested themes for a single group session or continue the theme for several sessions. A positive response from the members is your best clue to extend the theme. Some groups will be more stimulated by one theme than will another group. Don't rush to abandon a theme because it fizzles with one group. You can also repeat the theme in future groups with some changes or additions to the material or equipment. Leaders don't have to be encyclopedic experts on every group topic. Group members have taken delight in correcting the author's faulty assumptions about fishing, gardening, and driving a tractor. Their rush to champion what they know is a wonderful way to get even reluctant members involved in the group.

REMINISCENCE: FAVORITE VACATIONS

Goals: Recapture feelings of pleasurable leisure time. Members consider how their worldviews were changed by travel experiences.

Process: Group leader begins by telling a brief, humorous, or unique experience that occurred during a vacation. (If you have no such personal story, read a short essay or magazine article that sets the tone.) Ask each member to recall the location of his or her favorite vacation. The leader points to the place on a globe or adds a marker (pin-flag or sticker) on a map, then lets each member tell something about that vacation. Leader may prompt questions for sites, smells, sounds, weather, or people who were part of that vacation. If the group is suitable and the leader has appropriate professional training, guided imagery may be used to allow all members to feel the experience in their imaginations.

Outcomes: The best result is that members are refreshed from reexperiencing vacation or travel memories. As the locations are given, other members may recall having visited or lived in the same areas. Avoid excluding persons who have never traveled for pleasure. Encourage them to talk about whatever a unique, day-off-type experience was, even if it was riding the hay wagon into town monthly to shop. Institutionalized and community elders have so much free time that "leisure" is a burden. This group theme reminds them that leisure had a satisfying place in their life. Leaders need to listen for clues of personal interests pursued during leisure that may, in some way, be possible to duplicate now.

Equipment list: Globe or maps. Pin-flags or stickers. Essays or magazine articles about traveling or photos or pictorial travel brochures that show families, couples, and adults traveling.

REMINISCENCE: LIFELONG LEARNING

Goals: Discover how much each patient has learned over his or her life span. Identify ways that learning continues even in a restricted environment and with physical impairments. This group is better suited to higher functioning patients. Those with sight or hearing impairments or an inability to write can participate with assistance from another group member or a volunteer worker.

Process: Give each group member a pen and spiral notebook or sheets of lined paper with preprinted titles in a pocket folder. The leader needs a write-on board or overhead transparency projector and boldly colored markers. Begin each session with a quote or brief writing about learning. Create a group definition of learning with some free association of words that relate to learning. This theme easily fills four to six sessions without causing members to feel rushed and allowing after-group time to think about the subject. At each session, members discuss and write their feelings and recollections about these areas: first experiences of learning in elementary school; best and worst aspects of learning during formal education; skills learned on the job or in the home; things learned through hobbies, crafts, or sports; and important lessons learned from other people. A session may carry over to the next week if needed. Also, the leader may plan a wrap-up session to discuss overall feelings about this life review exercise and insights gained by each participant.

Outcomes: Learning is a sign of growth, progress, and achievement. As group members identify these elements of learning at various life stages, they find evidence of accomplishment and satisfaction. By probing for informal education experiences, even members who thought they had little education can take pride in what they have learned from living.

Equipment list: Pens, notebooks, or lined paper for each participant. Lap boards or tabletop for writing. Write-on board and boldly colored markers for the group leader.

REMINISCENCE: MY FIRST CAR

Goals: Driving and owning a car symbolizes independence, mobility, and fun. These factors are as important to elders as to teens. As each member recalls their part in the United States's fascination with the automobile, they reexperience a sense of control that is presently lost to them.

Process: The effective introduction was reading an essay from *Reminisce* magazine in which the author told of saving to buy a used Model T, working on it, and then the pride of taking his first drive around town. Male and female group members responded with recollections of saving and anticipating their first car. Show photos from books or magazines with cars from the 1920s, 1930s, 1940s, and 1950s and make a game of identifying the car manufacturer. Ask members to describe what driving or owning a car meant to their sense of independence, mobility, and fun. Allow members to talk about their last car and why they ceased to drive. Wrap up the final group session on this topic with an imaginary exercise. Using a write-on board or large poster board, the leader lists each member's name and transcribes the answers to each of these questions: If you awoke tomorrow with the physical ability to drive for 1 week and the money to buy any car you wanted, what kind of car would you buy and where would you drive?

Outcomes: Elders often silently mourn their loss of mobility, particularly in structured institutional care. Their generation saw dramatic changes in lifestyles related to the automobile. This topic can be both jovial and serious. Even cognitively impaired patients retain strong memories of their first cars and often can describe them in detail. A library book with reproductions of auto advertisements and slogans brought great delight, as did repetition of the manufacturers' slogans. In most geriatric groups, leaders need to redirect away from memories of auto accidents or other sad events. Work with those individuals separately outside of group.

Equipment list: Scan your public library for books on old cars and car advertisements. Model cars. Audiotapes of car advertisements. Contact the local antique car club for loan of these items or to drive by with a classic car. Markerboard or large poster board and boldly colored markers.

REMINISCENCE: CHILDHOOD GAMES

Goals: Games were an important part of entertainment both among children and with the family after dinner. Members recall the fun of the games and the times spent with their elders talking and bonding.

Process: Begin by talking about familiar childhood games. Invite each member to tell about his or her favorite game. The leader can prompt with questions about where, when, and with which friends or siblings these games were played. Discuss which childhood games members can still enjoy, such as checkers, dominoes, or cards. Talk about how their interest in games changed over time to such activities as board games, bridge, or chess. Relate how the ability to enjoy games and fellowship is ageless.

Outcomes: Recapturing memories of carefree evenings with family and friends shows how leisure time was prized and enjoyed. Games also bring back thoughts of spending time with childhood friends, family, and special parties.

Equipment list: Bring sample games such as jacks, dominoes, marbles, checkers, or jump rope. Ask the activity director which games are popular at the facility and bring in samples.

REMINISCENCE: BIRTHDAYS

Goals: Focus on celebrating life and the individual. A time for each member to reflect on which birthdays were most significant and why.

Process: This theme may be linked with a group member's birthday or on another day when the attention can be shared by all. Show and discuss the typical birthday party items and plans. Ask members to share any family traditions or ethnic customs for birthdays. Wrap a small gift box for each member. Inside place a card with a word or phrase explaining what you (the leader) wish for each member. Personal wish card needs to match the individual, such as joy, patience, laughter, or self-expression. Allow each member time to respond if he or she chooses. With prior approval from the nursing staff (or physicians), have traditional treats. Close the group by sharing a birthday cake. Put lots of candles on it and sing "Happy Birthday" to the group. This theme may also be repeated on an anniversary date of the group.

Outcomes: Less cohesive groups and cognitively impaired groups will benefit more from keeping this a lighthearted event. Groups dealing with adjustment issues can find comfort in celebrating their lives rather than taking a negative view of aging. Leaders must be aware of the reactions of severely depressed members who may fixate on a bad experience. Try to encourage recalling any pleasant birthday memory—if not their own, then those of their children, family, or friends. The overall purpose is to recall those times when aging was a desirable event and significant others celebrated their existence.

Equipment list: Birthday cake. If real cake is not allowed, there are fake cakes made from candles or fabric. Party hats and favors. Festive napkins and paper cups. Picture of children's parties. A history of birthday parties or ethnic parties book from the library. Small, wrapped gift boxes with personal wish cards inside.

REMINISCENCE: SEASONS OF THE YEAR

Goals: The changing of seasons has many meanings according to each individual's experiences. This aging cycle of nature becomes a metaphor for the life cycle, which is safer to discuss than human mortality, yet allows expression of feelings.

Process: This theme can be used quarterly at the beginning of each season or as an overview of all seasons. If all members have adequate dexterity, ask them to make a basic drawing of their favorite season. In presenting the picture to the group, encourage the artist to talk about the objects, scene, or choice of color and why it represents a certain season. Ask members what seasonal activities they recall doing during a certain season as children and as adults. Those who grew up on farms will have different memories than those who grew up in the city. Talk about traditional events that each person associates with a certain season, such as fall hayrides and harvest parties, snow and sledding in winter, first flowers of spring, and trips to the beach in the summer. Encourage vivid word pictures for the enjoyment of everyone. If the group seems ready for a deeper level, the leader introduces discussion about the planting, growing, harvesting, and completion of crops or flowers and how this relates to stages of life.

Outcomes: Seasons are about change and transition. The leader and group members can take this topic to a variety of levels depending on the group's capability and interest.

Equipment list: Color photos or posters that depict seasons. Local travel agents and elementary school teachers will have a wealth of seasonal material to loan. Bring typical seasonal items such as knitted gloves and hats, fall leaves, spring flowers, or a beach ball.

REMINISCENCE: THE KITCHEN

Goals: Stimulates memories of mothers and grandmothers, shared times around the table at meals, and times when food was a source of pleasure.

Process: As an elder woman shared, "The kitchen was the warmest place, not just because it had the big stove, but because the whole family gathered there." The kitchen is where many important mother–child interactions occurred. Ask each member to describe his or her favorite kitchen memory as a child. Who was there? What foods were cooking? What kitchen chore did they have? In later sessions, focus on the kitchen in each person's first home (after marriage or moving away from the family). If possible, locate a replica of an old appliance catalog. Read the descriptions of the kitchen products that were "new" 40 years ago. What was the most important modern appliance bought for their new kitchen? What do they think about frozen dinners, microwave ovens, and other devices that reduce the family's time together in the kitchen and at meals?

Outcomes: This home and hearth theme branches out in several directions from nostalgia to humor to memories of the family of origin. Any of these directions can provide a stimulating group discussion.

Equipment list: Look in the library section on historic homes and older editions of kitchen design for photos of earlier kitchens. A replica of an old appliance catalog (available at bookstores and some libraries). Bring models or dollhouse replicas of potbelly stoves, wringer washers, and newer stoves. Art paper and crayons or washable markers for writing.

REMINISCENCE: FAMILY GENOGRAM

Goals: Constructing a genogram is a simple overview of an individual's relationships and family heritage. This project celebrates continuity of life and the individual's role in the life chain. From this glimpse of the past, behavior patterns and family roles emerge that may be therapeutically significant in the here and now.

Process: The leader explains the concept of the genogram and shows several examples of well-known families in history, as found in McGoldrick and Gerson (1985). Focus attention on people, relationships, major events, and interesting or unusual information about people. Using a three-generation genogram form, have each group member be the second generation (middle) and chart their parental generation as the first generation and children or nieces and nephews as the third generation. This variation from the typical genogram process makes information retrieval easier and gives useful feedback on patients' relationships with adult children. To avoid frustration and memory blocks, eliminate dates. Divide the project into stages prepared during each group: introduce the topic; fill in the list of family names and relationships; fill in group members' generation, then add their parents' and children's generations; write in something special for each person if possible; list each person's occupation or hobby; and, finally, draw lines to indicate the nature of the relationships (close, conflictual, etc.). At a closing session, invite each member to present his or her own genogram to the group and discuss the most influential people in his or her life. The leader can make a transparency copy of each genogram for presentation on the overhead projector (larger and easier to read).

Outcomes: Genograms separate fact from fable by showing relationships in a concrete form. This method stimulates reassuring memories and shows unfinished business. What is learned about family patterns of scapegoating, dependency, and learned helplessness can be important in coping with present circumstances. A psychotherapist or psychologist as leader can choose to work with these intense feelings toward positive resolution. A leader with less training is advised to keep this theme on a lighter level and refer any members who are stuck in the emotional process for psychotherapy. Some of the therapeutic outcomes of genograms identified by Erlanger (1990) are similar to what has been seen in GSE groups: They take the focus off the patient's present problems, allow the patient to be the expert about him- or herself, and place the present into the total context of a lifetime.

(Continued next page)

Equipment list: A packet for each participant containing two blank genogram forms, family relationship form, key to genogram symbols, and sample complete genograms (it's best to print genogram form on 11-inch × 17-inch paper for easy reading). Pens. A lap board or tabletop for writing. Write-on board with boldly colored marker for the leader. Transparency projector with write-on markers to display the genogram format.

REMINISCENCE: DECADES OF LIFE

Goals: Gain a broad overview of life events and assign meaning to each decade.

Process: Leader introduces this approach to looking at life events within a 10-year context. Group members use one page for each decade of their lives to record personal information that is recalled from general discussion. Younger decades may be combined with a single-group session given for decades beyond middle age. A more detailed review results from a single session for each decade. The leader sparks each discussion with questions about the people, places, things, and events that were important during a stated decade. Members are asked to reflect on this information between sessions and be prepared to give a name or description for that period at the next group. When this project is complete, members will have a review of their life in segments and will have assigned meaning to each decade. Some titles used by members in previous groups to describe decades are 0–10, most cherished time; 21–30, becoming independent; 41–50, rediscovering our marriage; and 61–70, decade of loneliness. Encourage members to draw a scene, house, person, object, or anything that represents the decade description. This drawing is the introduction to the information sheets. Leaders assist members in compiling all sheets into a memory notebook.

Outcomes: Using the broader time segment of 10 years makes it easier for group members to recall significant events within a range. Unlike other types of life review that search for good and bad events of the past, this project focuses on the happy, productive, and satisfying events of each decade. With prompting and within the group discussion, each member will find something worth recalling at various ages. This project affirms the individual's connection to others over the life span.

Equipment list: Packet for each participant containing separate pages for each 10-year span (0–10, 11–20, 21–30, etc.); blank page for drawing with each decade printed at top, and scratch paper. Pens.

REMINISCENCE: LIFE INVESTMENT

Goals: Allow each member to reflect on how they "spent" their life to date and where they choose to "invest" future years.

Process: Leader introduces the concept of "investing" as the means of placing what is valuable to us in a way that gains a future return. Using a marker board and a marker, brainstorm with members for what *investing* and *return on investment* means to them in monetary terms. Then compare those terms with what they mean in personal terms with the days, creativity, and energy of their lives. In the second session, members are given a poster board with 10 columns. The last 2 are labeled *Today* and *My Future*. Members are asked to use scratch paper to list headings for the 8 other columns and discuss these as a group. Typical headings for life investment include spouse, children, grandchildren, work, church, sports, hobbies, military service, or community service. In the third session, each person must choose the headings for 8 columns that represent those places where she or he invested most of her or his life. The fourth session talks about how much each investment costs in terms of time, sacrifice, effort, and love. Using $100 in play money to represent a totality of life investment, members place amounts that signify their level of investment in each category. The only rule is that some investment must be "saved" for the Today and My Future headings. This activity may require two or three sessions. In the final session, invite members to share what they learned about their own life investment and whether, on reflection, there was a good return or inadequate return in their life or the lives of others. Discuss ways in which each

(Continued next page)

person can invest in the future of self and others in the group, family, or retirement community.

Outcomes: The investment concept is another tangible way to show how much of a person's life has been spent on self and others. This can lead to validation or more unfinished business and regrets. As previously mentioned, the depth of the negative emotional processing depends on the skill of the leader.

Equipment list: Play money from a toy store (or make play money using colored copier paper). An envelope for each participant. Small poster board with 10 columns drawn. Scratch paper. Marker board and boldly colored marker for leader.

Chapter 4

Bibliotherapy

Thus, gentle Reader, myself am the groundwork of my book.
—Michel de Montaigne, March 1, 1580

As French Renaissance essayist de Montaigne confessed, there is much about books and literary works that is personal, not just for the author, but also for the reader. The healing potential of the written word may have first been recognized by the ancient Thebans, who believed in the power of reading as a change agent (Schrank & Engels, 1981). Centuries later, therapists borrowed the same idea, called it bibliotherapy, and therein created a "new" treatment modality. The essence of bibliotherapy is in using written communication to probe thoughts, feelings, sensory perceptions, and abstract concepts for therapeutic purposes.

Popular press book publishers, newspaper advice columns, and personal experience articles continue to gain acceptance in the consumer market as a kind of nondirected, do-it-yourself bibliotherapy. Self-help books are among the most popular and cheaper means of dealing with life crises. The implementation of self-help in reading and following a program for behavioral change either alone or with a group has been useful in treatment of some psychological problems, notably alcoholism and anxiety (Glasgow & Rosen, 1978). Structured bibliotherapy requires more consideration in matching the individual's issues with meaningful, therapeutic reading. Bibliotherapy used as an element of the GSE group modalities is a structured, therapist-facilitated process with literary works chosen to enhance, challenge, or support the individual's work within the group.

Bibliotherapy is an exceptionally flexible modality that can be adjusted for high- to low-functioning groups as well as for persons with visual and hearing impairments. Use of this technique with geriatric groups is stylistically different than its traditional, more independent form. At one end of the spectrum is the pure self-help, self-selection that relies on comprehension, awareness of need to change, and implementation of change. The opposite end of that spectrum is highly directive, reader-assisted processing of information done with a therapist in individual or group work. The GSE groups, like many aging group programs, use a bibliotherapy approach that gives participants as much independence as possible yet enough assistance to maximize enjoyment and prevent frustration. Thus, structured bibliotherapy designed for the capabilities of each elder group is the context in which this modality is presented.

THERAPEUTIC BENEFITS

Reading about the emotions and difficult experiences of others provides a safe distance for processing feelings within an elder group. The candor that accompanies analysis of a fictional character's problems supersedes individual fears, guilt, or shame that sometimes inhibits ownership of problems (McKinley, 1977). This potential to recognize problems and solutions more easily when applied to fictional characters (than to self) is another reason that bibliotherapy is a useful treatment supplement for reducing depressive symptoms in elders with mild to moderate depression (Scogin, Hamblin, & Beutler, 1987). The magic of literature also allows readers to live vicariously through the author in experiences like hang gliding, traveling across Europe, playing a piano solo at Carnegie Hall, or dancing the night away. The limitations of mobility, dexterity, or finances cannot restrict the pleasures of armchair exploration through literature.

STAGES OF BIBLIOTHERAPY

Four distinct stages occur in geriatric group bibliotherapy: receive, perceive, believe, and weave. First, the group members must be able to receive the material, in either written or oral form. GSE prefers to use short written works such as essays, summaries, excerpts, or poetry. It is important to know the cognitive and reading skills of all participants. Retyping the material in large-print letters is appreciated by the group who prereads or follows along as the leader reads. Reading brief segments with a pause to recapture attention works best for lower functioning groups. By knowing the group members' reading skills, the leader can determine how to present the material so that all can receive it. Second, through discussion of the literature group members perceive the message. Higher functioning groups may delve deeply into the characters, situation, resolution, and alternatives as well as identify with a character. Lower functioning groups deal with the surface issues and basics of the story or feelings expressed by characters. Perceiving the bibliotherapy subject can be accomplished at whatever level the group operates. Even cognitively impaired groups, including Alzheimer's patients, can profit from bibliotherapy with therapist-directed discussion (Hynes & Wedl, 1990; Potenza & Labbancz, 1989). Third, participants need to believe in the significance, usefulness, emotional catharsis, or some message worth receiving that is derived from the literature. Concurrently, they must believe that they can apply the message in a personal way. Finally, there is the ability to weave what is learned or felt into the participant's self-concept.

COMPENSATING FOR LIMITATIONS

In traditional bibliotherapy in which the participant is solely responsible for keeping up with reading assignments and making oral or written reports, there is no provision for physical and mental impairments. Because these conditions are increasingly prevalent with aging adults, adjustments must be made for greater inclusion. Here are some suggestions that have proven effective in GSE groups.

1 For visually impaired elders, retype material in 24- or 36-point type, make a cassette recording of the material, or request a volunteer to read the material to the participant before group.

2 For hearing-impaired elders, place the participant close to the leader's right or left, whichever is the side of strongest hearing; check the participant's hearing aid for low batteries or other tuning; or print cue cards with key characters or discussion points to help the participant remain focused during the discussion.

3 For cognitively impaired elders, use brief, simple readings with fewer characters, read slowly, pause when group members disconnect and help them focus their attention, select literature with vivid word pictures and a crisp pace, consider using some children's literature with distinct characters and easy words.

4 For slow readers and nonreaders, avoid distinguishing them from the remainder of the group. If you give printed pages to others, also offer them to these participants; make a cassette recording of the material; or request a volunteer to read the material to the participant before group.

SELECTING LITERATURE FOR BIBLIOTHERAPY

As you will see from the items used in the GSE groups, almost any reading material, poem, essay, or prose can become the focal point of a structured bibliotherapy. A mixture of classics, contemporary, and historical works are generally appealing to elders. Depending on the group's interests, they may be willing to try current or less familiar works.

Remember your best ally in preparing bibliotherapy is a librarian! She or he is trained to match literature with the reading interests and levels of all ages. A university research librarian can give you background on the bibliotherapy concept and related journal articles. However, it's the librarian at the local public library who can keep your group well supplied with suitable material and suggest new acquisitions. Take time to talk with the local librarian to explain what is needed for your elder groups. You may also discover such treasures as the bookmobile or a local poetry reading that will visit your group on the librarian's recommendation.

BIBLIOTHERAPY: ENJOYING ESSAYS

Goals: Look at the simple things in new ways.

Process: The leader selects short (1- to 2-page) essays that highlight commonplace life experiences. A wealth of material is available in popular magazines such as *Reader's Digest* and *Guideposts* and the back pages of several women's magazines. Give each group member a copy to read before the next group or to follow along during the discussion. If possible, retype the essay using large-size type for easier reading. Recruit a volunteer from within the group to serve as the reader for visually impaired members. During the discussion, the leader uses a large marker board to track comments. Begin by asking each member what this essay communicated to them. Next, look at the style and tone of the writing. Finally, ask if anyone in the group relates to the writer's feelings or opinions. A high-functioning group may read at these deeper levels for discussion. However, a lower functioning group can also enjoy shorter (1-page) essays and talk about basic meanings.

Outcomes: Essays are regaining popularity by calling attention to simple things that are easily overlooked in a high-tech, excessively complex world. Elder groups who are so removed from the fast pace of today's society relate well to these glimpses of a slower, more peaceful time in their lives.

Equipment list: Copies of articles or essays from magazines, newspapers, or bound collections at the library. Marker board and boldly colored marker for leader.

BIBLIOTHERAPY: WHAT'S NEW IN OUR CITY (STATE OR NATION)?

Goals: Keeping up with current events

Process: A high-functioning group is encouraged to propose and agree on several themes that will be pursued during upcoming groups. The leader verifies that each member has access to newspapers or magazines at the facility or brings in a folder with precut articles. For example, if the group theme this month is to look at issues that face the city, then all articles discussed will relate to people or events occurring in the city. Each member is asked to report on an article or broadcast news report. The leader writes each major topic on the marker board. After each person gives a brief verbal report, the group may decide which issue to discuss further during the session. The leader may challenge the members to write their own letters to the editor or to send a group letter. To further bring the outside world inside, invite local newsmakers or news reporters to talk with the group. This opportunity to be in touch with people who influence the news is very stimulating to this type of higher functioning group.

Outcomes: This activity restores a sense of connectedness between the elder and the world outside present boundaries.

Equipment list: Clippings from local newspapers and news magazines. Marker board and boldly colored markers for leader.

BIBLIOTHERAPY: WHAT'S OLD IS NEW AGAIN

Goals: Linking the past with the present through social changes.

Process: A personal sense of aging is not numerically bound; rather, it's tied to the first time we say "That's not the way we used to do it." Many elders retreat into the mistaken belief that they are totally unconnected with today's society. This bibliotherapy activity demonstrates the recycling of social trends that continually link past and present. Using popular literature, the leader shares a "new" idea, such as the emphasis on family values, working at home to care for small children, or living simply. Group members discuss each topic and recall any related experiences. The leader may also bring in older writings that predicted the future such as George Orwell's *1984* or Jules Verne's *From the Earth to the Moon* and *Twenty Thousand Leagues Under the Sea*. When reading excerpts from such works, talk about how close these predictions came to reality. Invite group members to propose other topics showing how old ways are being revived as new.

Outcomes: Members gain a wider perspective by seeing themselves as part of a larger, fluid society with which they are not as out of touch as they may feel.

Equipment list: Newspaper or magazine articles about change and trends. A videotape or documentary about social trends. Library books.

BIBLIOTHERAPY: MYTHS AND FABLES

Goals: Examine how beliefs, superstitions, and legends emerged from ancient folk tales.

Process: The leader suggests several general topics, such as Greek mythology, Aesop's fables, Homer's *Odyssey, Analects* of Confucius, or Hans Christian Andersen fairytales and stories. The group selects a topic to read and discuss for 2 to 4 weeks. Excerpts are read aloud, with copies available to all members who desire to read the full work. The leader prepares large-type lists of questions for discussion. The group can be subdivided into teams or pairs to prepare comments on an assigned or chosen question. The initial discussions deal with the story, characters, setting, and moral of the story. Some groups may want to dig deeper by probing for feelings about the situation, story resolution, and comparable circumstances that individuals have faced.

Outcomes: This is a rediscovery of favorite stories or a new look at the origin of beliefs, superstitions, and legends that were accepted knowing the source.

Equipment list: Library books. Pictorial history books that show people and places in the time period of the reading material.

BIBLIOTHERAPY: FORGET TV SHOPPING, GET MY CATALOG!

Goals: This is a nostalgic view of dreams and wishes from the past.

Process: The leader introduces the topic by asking members to recall the best (and worst) items they purchased by mail order. Talk about the thrill of discovery in the advertisement, the anticipation of awaiting delivery, and the satisfaction or dissatisfaction with the item ordered. Sharing these stories will bring out a range of feelings from humor to frustration. At the next group, display copies of old catalogs or catalog replicas. Let each member select two favorite items to share with the group. Read aloud the descriptions. Compare the quality, prices, and features of the old catalog items to similar newer items. Typically, you will find that several members recall ordering certain items and can discuss the experience in detail. At the next session, bring weekend newspaper ads for similar items at department and hardware stores. Look at the differences in items and advertising descriptions. Talk about how malls are intended to replace main street storefronts and whether group members agree with that objective. As a summary group, tune into a TV shopping channel to see and hear how items are sold in this video catalog approach. Discuss how the armchair shopping convenience of catalogs yielded to the malls and is back again with TV shopping.

Outcomes: Using the common experience of shopping, delve into the changing methods of acquisition and how the newest trend resembles the old method. This activity is fun and a springboard for reminiscence with high and low functioning groups.

Equipment list: Replicas of catalogs and advertisements from several time periods after the 1900s. Weekend newspaper ads.

BIBLIOTHERAPY: ATTITUDES ABOUT AGING

Goals: Expand perspectives on aging and seek positive input.

Process: The leader presents a text (book, collection of essays or short stories) as a basis for discussion. Taking brief segments of a book or a single essay or short story, read aloud, with members following along on copies. Effective material covers a variety of aspects of aging: health, loss, mobility, adult children, grandchildren, friends, retirement, money, changes in activities, worry, change, and expectations. Discuss the situation and the writer's viewpoint. Does the group agree or offer alternative coping strategies? How can such a situation be turned into a positive? What advice would the group offer? In brainstorming such questions to benefit a third party, group members can tackle difficult issues that are too sensitive to personalize.

Outcomes: Talking about aging issues at this distance gives more freedom of expression to test ideas before claiming them for oneself.

Equipment list: Book with poems, essays, or short stories. One favorite of GSE groups is *Old Is Older than Me* by Maxine Dowd Jensen.

BIBLIOTHERAPY: RHYME ME A RHYME

Goals: Find meaning and expression in poetry.

Process: With high-functioning groups, the leader involves members in selecting a type of poem, specific poet, or period of poetry to read and study. Newly formed groups and lower functioning groups benefit from the leader selecting well-known works such as Walt Whitman's *Leaves of Grass* or Edgar Allan Poe's "The Raven." After reading the poem aloud, discuss its feelings, images, and mood. For groups who genuinely enjoy poetry, introduce some different styles of verse for other cultures such as Spanish *coplas* (couplets), the *Rubaiyat of Omar Khayyam*, or Rabindranath Tagore's "Fireflies."

Outcomes: Poetry is another means of reaching feelings and becomes a focal point for expressing those feelings.

Equipment list: Books of poetry.

BIBLIOTHERAPY: ARMCHAIR EXPLORING

Goals: Launch an adventure that transcends physical boundaries.

Process: The leader gives each member an invitation rolled up as a scroll with map and treasure symbols. Inside is a brief description of the journey that the group will follow with literature, pictures, and maps. Select a vivid and varied experience such as Homer's *Odyssey* or Marco Polo's travels. Discuss the planned route and show the area on a globe or map. If possible, pin up a map so that reading progress can be marked at each session. Divide the literary work into segments for reading aloud. Provide copies as requested. Discuss each episode, the critical event, the result, and what was learned by overcoming that obstacle. Encourage members to project themselves to that time and place as if they were members of the fictional exploration team.

Outcomes: Stimulates the imagination and creative thinking while providing a healthy escape from present circumstances.

Equipment list: Books, globe, map. Historical books with pictures of people, costumes, and places help set the mood.

BIBLIOTHERAPY: CHILDHOOD RHYMES

Goals: Examine the words, meanings, and historical roots of familiar nursery rhymes.

Process: The leader gives members a copy of a familiar nursery rhyme (or distributes different rhymes to each member). Well-known rhymes to read and discuss are "Mary, Mary Quite Contrary," "Humpty Dumpty," "London Bridge," "Little Jack Horner," "Ring Around the Rosie," "Little Miss Muffet," and "Twinkle, Twinkle, Little Star." After reading each rhyme aloud, discuss its meaning. Is this a rhyme to entertain or teach a principle to children? Does anyone know the historical background of the rhyme? The leader makes discussion notes on the marker board. Where information exists on the history and political overtones of a rhyme, share these with the group. Some rhymes were disguised social and political comments applicable to their times. The group can use this idea to recreate rhymes with modern figures; for example, "Mary, Mary Quite Contrary" is about more than a garden growing. Are there members of any present royal families whose behavior is quite contrary? Is there a political figure who is poised for a great fall, like Humpty Dumpty? Or is this metaphor applicable to the fall of the Soviet Union, split into too many parts to put together again? Write down the results of the group's creative thinking.

Outcomes: Here is another way to look deeper into seemingly simple words. Rhymes are reminiscent of childhood and parenting years. Higher functioning groups can complete the full range of this activity. Lower functioning groups relate to these rhymes and discussion about how they are a part of childhood.

Equipment list: Books of children's rhymes and their meanings, with copies for the group. Look in the library for reproductions of early classics, such as *Mother Goose's Rhymes* (1760/1980). Marker board and boldly colored markers for the leader.

BIBLIOTHERAPY: THE CROSSROADS OF OUR LIVES

Goals: Reflect on the major choices and circumstances that altered the direction of life and recognize long-held beliefs about those crossroads experiences.

Process: The leader or group members read aloud Robert Frost's poem "The Road not Taken." With this classic metaphor for life crisis, begin by asking each group member to share how one choice affected his or her life for the better and another for the worse. Give each person full attention in a kinder version of the Gestalt "hot-seat" method wherein the leader and group members ask questions with the intent of identifying each individual's strengths. The leader lists strengths that the individual and group hear in reviewing the personal story and transcribes a list of those strengths to give to each person. If this group takes additional sessions, begin each time by reading Frost's poem to set the mood. This activity may become more psychotherapeutic and therefore more appropriate for psychotherapists or psychologists as leaders. If facilitated by other health professionals or used with lower functioning groups, read the poem and steer discussion to the positive choices and good decisions of life rather than the traumatic events.

Outcomes: This exercise is a type of life review with poetry as basis. It can become very intense or remain limited to surface emotions, depending on the group's willingness to participate. At any level, this exercise airs and gives structure to the tendency to ruminate over roads taken and chances missed.

Equipment list: "The Road not Taken," a poem by Robert Frost. Write-on board and markers for the leader.

Chapter 5

Exploring Values and Roles

The creation and preservation of values; that is what gives meaning to our civilization, and the participation in this is what gives significance, ultimately, to the individual human life.

—Lewis Mumford

A meaningful element of life satisfaction is derived from the roles we have filled and the values we hold dear. Each group member arrives with a collection of established values and roles (both positive and negative). These long-held attitudes and personal experiences form the basis for this modality of self-discovery and social interaction. Regardless of how many values or roles are shared or different, themes emerge that are integral to reinforce self-esteem. Exploring values and roles is a reflective, existential modality that searches for meaning from the past as a sustaining force for a time-limited and uncertain future.

VALUES

The significance of values as an expression of unity between the mind and the heart was recognized by John Dewey (1939). Years later, the quest was revived by Maslow (1959) and Rogers (1961) as important to the psychosocial development of each person. In looking at the origin of values, Piaget (1965) explained that the earliest childhood encounter with value development comes in two stages: *moral realism,* the reality of rules, and *moral relativism,* the potential to change rules. Kohlberg (1963) expanded Piaget's stages into a theory of moral development with three levels (premoral, role conformity, and self-accepted morality) and seven stages. The stages in the third level constitute an ongoing series of decisions about individual rights, dictates of conscience, and individual actions as part of a universal ethic. Bathed in the afterglow of the humanist movement, Raths, Hamin, and Simon (1966) created a controversial approach known as *values clarification* to be used in schools. As the popularity of values clarification grew, its application expanded to include adults from corporate team building to a less academically inclined method of teaching courses intended to loosely resemble philosophy.

This modality is an adaptation of values clarification with elders that might better be called *values solidification*. Among Raths et al.'s (1966) criteria for a clarified value are that it be cherished, claimed publicly, and consistently practiced. GSE groups begin with the assumption that senior adults have enough life experience to know what they consider their values to be. Even cognitively impaired elders retain much of their values or life rules in a very concrete way, although they may no longer be able to deal with the information in an abstract, philosophical manner. Regardless of formal education, the present senior adult generation has far less difficulty articulating their values than do their baby boomer children. Elders in our geriatric groups are products of the work ethic, with a self-reliant, can-do creed. Work with them to identify and recapture the positive feelings emanating from adherence to those values.

ROLES

For many elders, who you are and what you do are synonymous. Job descriptions were short and simple for persons coming of age for work in post-Depression America. There were white-collar industrialists, blue-collar laborers, soil-collared farmers, and homeless persons who lost both shirts and collars. Women were primarily the white-gloved ladies of the house or their white-aproned servants. Workers, predominately men, found a job with the goal of a secure paycheck and receiving a gold watch at retirement. In a similarly structured style, relationships were predictable. The social rules dictated a lifelong monogamous marriage with children. Grandparents were treated with profound respect and were often cared for in the homes of their adult children. This was a time in which family values were prized and most people were in agreement about the nature of those values. Coming from such a predictable social order, today's elders must feel like Dorothy, hit by a ton of bricks and wondering if they are in Kansas. The rigid role definitions that they expected seem to vanish at the time they enter a bewildering period that Blau (1973) called *role exit*. Stable patterns of socialization and meaning cease. The elder is no a longer a parent, coworker, or resident of the same neighborhood. Add to that the deaths of a spouse and of family or friends, and the individual faces a series of losses that rip apart lifetime attachments. New roles emerge, yet even those roles are often restricted by mobility, illness, isolation, and financial reversal. The geriatric group leader must understand the significance of roles in the life of elders. There are many strengths and characteristics to be discovered about the roles of a lifetime. An 70-year-old man comes to mind who insisted that he had "never amounted to anything." During an exploration of values and roles, he found a side of himself that he had never before recognized. He had long "felt guilty staying home with his mother and sisters during World War II." In reality, he was the only male left at home to help support the family, as his father had been killed in the early months of fighting and his three older brothers had enlisted. As the group talked about what kinds of things he did every day and how he helped his family, a different picture developed. He finally acknowledged that he had been the man of the house, keeping the roof repaired and working extra hours to buy his sister's graduation dress. Seeing this critical young adult role as important was key to looking at the positive aspects of subsequent life roles.

VALUES AND ROLES FOR THE GROUP

At a time when roles are diminishing for elders, membership in the group becomes a new role that is tailored to present circumstances. Understanding the values and roles that have sustained an elder to this point provides important clues to effective coping in aging. Looking for elements of life satisfaction and current ability to deal with aging are part of restoring or discovering a new level of self-esteem. This is an intense process from which the most lasting results are derived by groups with greater levels of cohesion. In a less intense application, this is suitable as an anchor and redirection modality for cognitively impaired groups.

There is no attempt to change or challenge values unless the elder makes that decision independently. Efforts at values solidification are to have each member identify, claim, and find new ways to apply personal values to present living. Along with exploring past roles and the positive elements therein, members are discovering new roles within the group. Highly cohesive groups are particularly amazing in how they create group roles. One very special GSE group decided to redefine their group roles as a family. The oldest man (94) and the oldest woman (92) received consensus as the "parents." The members in their 80s were their children and two ladies in their 90s felt best as "aunties." Because of her relative youth, a 66-year-old woman became the "baby sister." In case you are wondering what happened to the 30-something group leaders, they were designated "friends." This role assignment surfaced periodically and playfully in a way that all seemed to enjoy. When the baby sister suffered a stroke, her group family showered her with concern and visits. This "role adaptation" was the first of many signs that the new roles in group filled Grand-Canyon-sized voids in these people's desire to care about others. If there are such things as dream teams, then this was the "dream geriatric group experience." They enacted Yalom's (1985) belief that the best curative factors in group therapy emerge from the support, acceptance, and hope generated within the group rather than from any therapeutic magic of the leader.

ROLE: BIRTH ORDER

Goals: Consider an individual's role in the family of origin according to birth order.

Process: The leader introduces the topic by asking each group member about the number of siblings and his or her placement in the birth order. Write this information on the marker board (i.e., Mary—third child, first girl). As framework for the discussion, the leader reads segments of literature on birth order, roles, and personality types. A prewritten poster in large lettering giving brief characteristics of only child, first child, middle child, and youngest child is a helpful reference tool for members. Each member is asked to comment on how she or he conforms to the birth-order assumptions. The discussion can expand to include perceptions of parental favoritism or scapegoating of different siblings.

Outcomes: Birth-order theories are unfamiliar to many elders and generate insights about their place within the family and that of their siblings.

Equipment list: Reference books on birth order, such as *Understanding Yourself Through Birth Order* or *The Birth Order Factor: How Your Personality is Influenced by Your Place in the Family.* Poster board charts. Marker board and boldly colored markers.

ROLE: BELIEFS ABOUT FAMILIES

Goals: Elders have experienced several generations of family life: their grandparents, parents, children, and grandchildren. This topic deals with the imperatives and beliefs about family life and how they have been manifested in several generations.

Process: Leader begins with a discussion of what constitutes a family. As group members formulate this definition, they are asked to describe the ideal family. The leader adds sociological information on how the definition of family has changed during this century by reading about traditional families, blended families, divorced families, single-parent families, adoptive families, and transracial and transcultural families. Members are then asked about how their families changed from their grandparents' generation through that of their adult children and grandchildren. Has anything changed in their families' definition of the role of elder relatives? In society's definition? Is the role of family matriarch or patriarch the same as it was for prior generations? How does each member feel about the changes?

Outcomes: Family beliefs about roles are significant to the way elders are treated. If the family respect for elders diminished over generations, then the present elders may feel cheated and angry. If the elder role is revered, then there is comfort and respect. Dealing with these feelings is too often minimized by family and caregivers.

Equipment list: None.

ROLE: BEST FRIENDS

Goals: To recapture positive feelings of sharing with friends.

Process: The leader begins by reading a short essay on friendship or telling a positive personal story of an experience with a best friend. Members are given a few quiet moments to recall the friendships that enhanced their lives and tell about their best friends and what made the relationships special. The leader tracks names and comments as each person speaks (i.e., Mark—childhood friend, played baseball together, got measles at same time). These comments can also be recorded by or for the member on individual pages. After everyone has a turn discussing a best friend, ask members to reflect on a person that they decided to befriend and how this was accomplished. With higher functioning groups, talk about the risks and benefits of making new friends at this time in life. Brainstorm a plan for approaching another resident and beginning a friendship.

Outcomes: Family is a given, friends are chosen. The persons, circumstances, and results of friendships are indelible experiences from which elders can draw strength and recall feelings of acceptance.

Equipment list: Short essay on friendship. Marker board. Paper and pen.

ROLE: WORK OR CAREER

Goals: Look at the importance of work or career in adult life and how to deal with the loss of that role in retirement.

Process: Before group, the leader reads social histories of each member to learn something about prior occupations. Bringing photos or props that symbolize those occupations enhances the discussion. The leader begins this topic by recalling the Horatio Alger work ethic on which most elders were raised. Discuss what the work ethic means to each member. Then become more specific, asking each member to recall his or her first job. What were the duties and where and how much was the pay? Who was influential in selecting the type of work (the individual, parents, spouse, teacher?) What type of work was pursued in later years? What was the last job before retirement? How did work outside and inside the home change during their work years? Do they miss working? If each person could return to work now and get any job imaginable, what would that job be? What skills would that job require? High- and low-functioning groups participate well in discussions about work and hold strong feelings about personal productivity linked to the work ethic.

Outcomes: Probing experiences and attitudes toward work tells much about self-image in older adults. The imaginary work question may give clues to activities or skills that an individual may be able to translate into leisure activities.

Equipment list: Occupational photos and props (i.e., firefighter's hat, chalkboard, briefcase, toolbox, or chef's apron).

ROLE: PARENTING OR CARETAKING

Goals: Consider the importance of being needed as parent or caretaker.

Process: The leader asks each member to name his or her children or another person for whom he or she had caretaking responsibilities. Discuss the role of parent or caretaker. Ask each member what qualities define a good parent or caretaker. Which of those qualities did they develop while parenting or caretaking? What were the changes in their roles as adults, workers, or spouses that occurred because of parenting or caretaking? Were those changes anticipated or resented? Did they model their roles after their parents or choose to change how they fulfilled parenting or caretaking roles? What caretaker in their life now is most like their ideal caretaker role and why? How do they show appreciation to this good caretaker? Encourage the group to list on the marker board ways to verbally reward good caretaking and appropriately express views of inadequate care.

Outcomes: Moving from the elders' parenting or caretaking roles to expectations and realities about care-receiving can aid adjustment to the present situation and identification rather than hostility toward caregivers.

Equipment list: Marker board.

ROLE: ACTIVITIES IN THE COMMUNITY

Goals: Review how individuals became invested in the larger community and the results of their participation.

Process: The leader displays a poster with concentric circles labeled from the center outward: self, family, neighborhood, school, church, interest group, and city. Bring the poster to each member, point to each circle, and ask members to tell one way to be involved in each area. Talk about the type of activities and level of commitment and satisfaction gained from each activity. Encourage members to compare activities and different ways of contributing to similar aspects of community. In a later or expanded group, discuss present opportunities to participate in their community through residents' council, interest groups, or outside activities.

Outcomes: Recognizing the desire of emotionally healthy adults to participate in a community outside of self and family, motivate members to be as invested as possible in the community within their reach.

Equipment list: Marker board and poster illustration.

ROLE: CLICHÉS AS IMPERATIVES

Goals: Elders grew up with many clichés given as rules. Explore how influential these clichés were in their beliefs and definition of roles.

Process: The leader writes several well-known clichés on the marker board, such as "A stitch in time saves nine," "Still waters run deep," "Don't cry over spilt milk," and "If at first you don't succeed, try, try, try again." Members are asked to recall other clichés that they frequently heard or said. After collecting additional statements, ask members to explain in their own words what each cliché means. Discuss differences in meaning. Does the statement express a moral or practical message? How is it used? Are some clichés regional or ethnic in origin? Which clichés reflect or define personal beliefs?

Outcomes: Clichés are a former generation's "shoulds" that restrict behaviors and state imperatives. This exercise encourages thinking about how clichés defined an individual's role and beliefs and whether they remain valid for today.

Equipment list: Marker board or preprinted posters. Large-print copies for each member to follow.

ROLE/VALUE: RULES TO LIVE BY

Goals: Determine how rules were defined, assimilated, and transmitted to individuals and the impact of rules for role definition.

Process: The leader begins with a simple definition of rules and gives several common examples for rules of conduct, for example, the 10 Commandments, the Golden Rule, the Good Samaritan, public laws, and Civil Rights legislation. Members are asked to name other rules that governed their conduct in their parental home as children and later as adults. The leader lists answers on the marker board. From among the rules listed, each member is given time to tell which were most influential in his or her life and why. This discussion can be expanded to include such topics as which rules did they find fair or unfair in their lives, who made the rules in their homes, how do they feel about the rules that affect them in the present circumstances, and what can they do to change or cope with the rules if they disagree?

Outcomes: Elders are typically a rule-respecting generation, however, that does not imply agreement with rules. This topic allows a nonjudgmental forum to discuss feelings about rules that governed past and present life.

Equipment list: Marker board.

ROLE: THE GOOD NEIGHBOR

Goals: In less frantic times, neighbors were a vital part of the family social circle and the primary source of adult interaction for homemakers. This exercise reflects on the role of neighbors and how to recapture it.

Process: The leader begins by reading an essay or showing a video segment of a classic family-oriented show with a positive scene of communication between neighbors. Members are invited to recall and tell of a favorite neighbor. What was special about that person? How did this neighbor help the member's adjustment to a new area? Next, ask how each member acted as a good neighbor to someone else. Discuss the qualities of a good neighbor, which the leader summarizes on the marker board. For higher functioning groups, refocus this topic to present circumstances. How can they be a good neighbor to another resident in a retirement or nursing home? What can they do with limited resources and mobility to show that they are good neighbors? Would they think differently about living in this facility if they considered it their new neighborhood?

Outcomes: At all levels, members can find satisfaction in recollections of having or being a good neighbor. Challenge higher functioning groups to find ways to bring the good-neighbor concept to present circumstances.

Equipment list: Essay on or videotape of a classic family-oriented show. Marker board.

ROLE: THE ROLES OF MY LIFE

Goals: After conducting several role-oriented group topics, this topic crystallizes each person's self-image as influenced by the roles he or she has played in life.

Process: The leader reviews prior group discussions on roles. In creating a list of roles for each person, either work separately to list each person's roles or list key roles and names of each member acknowledging that role. Stimulate recall with basic roles divided by age or stage, for example, member as a youth was child, grandchild, niece or nephew, student, friend, or teammate. In adulthood, roles may include friend, dating partner, spouse, worker, homemaker, business owner, aunt or uncle, and parent. Some later adult roles are friend, grandparent, widow or widower, club member, and retiree. Draw out special interests that add other roles such as artist, sewer, carpenter, cook, gardener, or photographer. Make a list of roles for each person. Even those with low self-esteem who claim to have done nothing important are surprised at how many roles they have filled in life. With higher functioning groups, expand this topic to discuss ways to amplify or alter present roles. A leader who is aware of community resources and facility programs can help members connect with additional means of role fulfillment.

Outcomes: This is an effective self-esteem-building exercise for those at all levels of functioning.

Equipment list: Marker board and personal inventory sheets.

Chapter 6

Sensory Awareness

Some feelings are quite untranslatable; no language has yet been found for
them. —H. W. Longfellow

With aging and physical limitations come fewer opportunities for sensory stimulation as caregivers seek to make the environment safe. This loss of tactile contact combined with declining sensory perceptions creates a bland world. The
sensory pleasures of sight, sound, smell, taste, and touch diminish in aging adults
more as a result of apathy than of lack of ability. Inherent in the protection and
safety issues of residential senior housing is the reduction of opportunities to
engage the senses. Meals are prepared in a restricted-access kitchen and served
without the elders' having the enjoyment of smelling the food as it cooks. That's
just one of many ways elders in residential care become removed from common
sensory experiences and dependence on sensory perception.

RESTORING SENSORY ENJOYMENT

Restoring whatever degree of sensory enjoyment is possible for the elder group is
yet another comforting connection with the familiar, enjoyable experiences of the
past. The key to communicating with elders who have cognitive or speech
impairments can be through sensory awareness with the alternative of nonverbal
responses. Bryant (1991) found that creative approaches to the sensory awareness group makes therapy viable for persons who cannot otherwise participate
effectively in verbal, task-oriented groups. McMurray (1989) noted that painting
and clay modeling used in art therapy have the added bonus of increasing sensory
stimulation.

GSE groups encourage the use of senses to the fullest extent possible for each participant. No assumptions are made on the basis of physical limitations. For example, an elder with severe arthritis may not be able to hold a velvet scarf and discern the texture with her hands. With the elder's permission, try placing the velvet scarf on her arm or against her cheek where there may be greater sensory awareness. If tactile sensation or vision is limited, approach the senses with vivid word pictures. The touch of silk communicates soft. Descriptions such as "like baby's skin, a feather pillow, or fluffy cotton balls" also give the impression of soft without touching an object.

CHILDREN

Another way to expand sensory awareness activities is to watch children around the home. What unexpected things bring squeals of delight? Soap bubbles, digging in the garden, and making doll-sized pies from dough scraps. Children gravitate toward sensory activities, adults ignore them, and elders are restricted from them. Sensory experiences are small pleasures to be enjoyed by all ages, not just by children.

SENSORY ACTIVITY: BACK TO NATURE

Goals: The feel of soil, beauty of flowers, and satisfaction of being involved in something that is alive and thriving.

Process: Choose a spring or fall time that is suitable for conducting this group outside. Set up on picnic tables or card tables for all members. Distribute supplies to members' "workstations" before they arrive. After each member is seated, offer a choice of two plants to repot. Open group with a review of the steps for this project. State each step simply. Prepare a one-page instruction sheet of the steps for high-functioning persons. If this is a low-functioning group, take each step slowly and wait until everyone finishes before beginning the next step. While working, either (a) initiate a discussion of prior gardening experiences or (b) go around to each person and ask them to describe this experience. The leader makes certain that each plant is labeled. On one side of a small, flat stick (such as a tongue depressor or Popsicle stick), write the plant's name and on the other side write the member's name. Depending on the preferences of the facility, growing plants may not be permitted in the patients' rooms. The leader can place all plants in a larger box and tend them outside. These growing plants can be brought back in a few weeks to admire, enjoy, touch, and discuss the pleasure of being part of their growing process.

Outcomes: The first time GSE used this activity, the results were amazing. Even the most sullen, withdrawn man in group became as animated as a laser light show. He dug joyfully in the dirt, finished his plants, then spontaneously offered to help other members. When asked how he felt doing this activity, he responded, "I'm touching the good earth where life is. Do you know they never let us get dirty around here?" This activity is another example of how the cleanliness necessary for an assisted living home means some loss of simple pleasures like digging around flowers. Over the years, most of our group members had either lived at some time on a farm or visited relatives on farms. Planting, gardening, and working

(Continued next page)

with nature are familiar and comforting for many elders. This activity is a springboard for reminiscences with some groups; for others it is a nonverbal, very sensual experience.

Equipment list: Small bedding plants purchased 4–6 per grouping. Potting soil. Plastic scoops or spoons. Small clay pots or recycled margarine tubs. Popsicle sticks or physician's tongue depressors. Enough supplies for each participant to have two completed plantings. One-page instruction sheet.

SENSORY ACTIVITY: BAKING PARTY

Goals: Recreate the sights, sensations, smells, and enjoyment of baking bread.

Process: This takes prior coordination from the facility or careful planning if used with nonresidential community groups. Each member begins by cleaning his or her hands and getting seated at workstations. With larger tables, seat 3–4 people per table. They form a group within the group for discussion while the project is underway. Let each person grease a small pan, knead the dough, and form a loaf in the pan. Write names or initials on each pan. As these return to the kitchen to rise and bake, clean up the work areas. The leader initiates a discussion about this activity or lets the group move toward reminiscences of bread baking at other times. As members share feelings or memories, the leader prompts for more sensory information. The next day or at the next group, return the completed bread to be admired and eaten.

Outcomes: Smells, sounds, sights, and tastes of home baking are frequently associated with significant times (childhood, first home) and special people (mother, wife, friend). All of those senses are recaptured in this activity along with potential for reminiscence and fellowship at the work tables.

Equipment list: The facility dietary kitchen prepares bread dough ready for kneading. Small disposable bread pans or cupcake tins. Tables covered for use in kneading the bread. Several plastic containers.

SENSORY ACTIVITY: A BIT OF FLORIDA SUNSHINE

Goals: Enjoy the color, smell, feel, and taste of peeling and eating oranges.

Process: Here's a simple activity that combines several sensory elements in sharing conversation while peeling and eating fresh oranges. As group members are peeling the oranges, the leader asks each person to take time to smell and touch the fruit and asks each to try to find something new about it that he or she has never noticed before. Florida orange growers say their crop comes from the sunshine tree. Engage the group in a discussion about what brings "sunshine" into their lives or recall memories of picking and eating fruit fresh from the source. If weather permits, conduct group outside or save this activity for a cold winter day when changing the focus to a sunshine theme may reduce those seasonal doldrums.

Outcomes: The use of various senses is rivaled by the sheer pleasure of the activity. Some members with arthritis or other digital impairments may need assistance getting started. The leader needs to prompt members to help each other and enjoy the fellowship. This is a messy yet tactile experience that is suitable for all group levels (subject to dietary approval).

Equipment list: Fresh oranges. Plastic, rimmed plates or bowls. Lots of napkins.

SENSORY ACTIVITY: SOLVE THE MYSTERY
WITHOUT LOOKING

Goals: Stimulate connections between thinking and touch or smell to identify an object.

Process: Before group, the leader prepares a collection of items that may be identified by touch or smell. Higher functioning groups may enjoy making a game of this by pairing members or dividing into teams. Cheer on each team as they use their sensory perception to solve the most mystery items. Here are some items that are effective in this exercise. In small canisters, saturate cotton balls with peppermint oil, rose oil, lemon, vanilla extract, or perfume or use a small piece of strong onion. In separate paper bags, place a hairy kiwi fruit, pinecone, sponge, bar of soap, small potato, and lettuce leaf. As each person is trying to name the mystery item by smell or feel, prompt him or her to describe the item. After everyone has a turn, the leader can reveal the mystery items. This sensory activity can prompt a game-like atmosphere with lots of laughter and fun. Note: For lower functioning groups, go around the room with items on a tray and let each person select one mystery item. Engage the attention of the others as each person tries to describe the mystery item with the leader's assistance.

Outcomes: Exploring common items in a nonvisual way stimulates the senses to support the process. This is particularly enjoyed by persons with impaired eyesight who are not receiving ample opportunities to motivate their other senses.

Equipment list: Clean, recycled black plastic film canisters. Paper bags. Fresh fruits and other mystery items.

SENSORY ACTIVITY: WE'RE FOREVER BLOWING BUBBLES

Goals: Sensory experiences with touch and sight.

Process: Gather the group outside. The leader begins by blowing bubbles. It's the rare elder group in which someone won't break into song about "forever blowing bubbles". If you can find a recording, play it on tape or lead the group in singing a cappella. Then give bubble bottles to each member and invite them to join. Direct their attention to the form, size, and rainbow colors that appear in the light. The leader takes a cue from the group's comments for a discussion of bubbles as either metaphors for personal dreams and wishes or fun memories of blowing bubbles with their children.

Outcomes: This carefree activity is a pleasant break between more serious topics in a multisession program or as an introductory session with a new group.

Equipment list: Small bubble containers are inexpensive in multipacks at some toy stores. Cassette tape of bouncy, lighthearted instrumental music.

SENSORY ACTIVITY: FACE UP

Goals: Getting to know oneself on a nonvisual level.

Process: The leader opens with comments (or reads a light verse) on how people see themselves. The group is challenged to see themselves in a new way by exploring their own faces without looking in a mirror. The leader models each step. Begin by using the hand used least often (i.e., a right-handed person uses the left hand). With fingers together and spread flat, touch the fingertips to each part of the face while describing the feel to both your fingers and your face. Make the exercise even more interesting by repeating it with eyes closed. In a clockwise motion, lightly touch and tap in this order: forehead, cheek, chin, under chin, cheek, nose, and lips. Then repeat the procedure using the opposite hand and determine if the feel to fingers or face is different.

Outcomes: Along with tactile focus, this sensory activity places attention on the individual as worthy of exploring and on knowing more about the self.

Equipment list: None.

SENSORY ACTIVITY: THE SENSATIONS OF COLOR

Goals: Associating colors with sights, sounds, smells, and touch.

Process: The elder generation was raised on the nonvisual imagery of classic radio programs. In a similar manner, this sensory exercise seeks to stimulate images or tell a story using other senses. Work with one primary color at a time to focus concentration. For example, the leader begins by talking about the color red. Give each member a piece of red paper or red fabric as a reference during this activity. Point out other reds in the room. Ask each member to tell one thing that reminds them of red. Then play a tape or make "red" sounds such as a fire siren (red truck, red in fire), a bold trumpet note (red as brassy), or tires screeching (putting on brakes). Show red objects (red pepper, beach ball, toy fire truck, etc.). Inquire if anyone associates red with any strong smells, tastes, or touches. Talk about how each person feels when surrounded by the color red. The leader can read short items from color psychology literature or decorating books on the types of persons attracted to red. Continue as long as the group is involved before proceeding to explore another color and repeat the exploration. Colors stimulate vivid images and feelings for at least some group members.

Outcomes: The full range of senses are probed in relation to colors. Eyesight is not critical to this activity. As long as the person has experienced colors, he or she can participate well. One of GSE's oldest group members who had long ago lost her eyesight as a result of illness greatly enjoyed "the colors thing." Her imagination and enthusiasm for relating feelings to colors was extraordinary.

Equipment list: Tape of sound effects (look in library or request assistance from a local radio station). Any other sound-producing items (e.g., toys, bells, household items). Sound-book toys have wonderful audio images. Box of primary color crayons, colored paper, or colored fabric. Books about color psychology literature or decorating books such as *Color Psychology and Color Therapy* by Birren, *The Psychology of Color and Design* by Sharpe, or "Role of Color in Perception of Attractiveness" by Radeloff.

SENSORY ACTIVITY: FUR AND FEATHERS—PET VISITS

Goals: Combines touch with enjoyment and memories of animals.

Process: Several days before group, be certain that no member is afraid of or allergic to the animals that will visit. If so, offer that member the choice to remain outside group or join another activity. For an in-depth study of pets as therapy, review the literature. GSE's most successful pet activities involved visits from a large, gentle dog who later came to live at the facility. A GSE therapist brought several sizes of parrots and, the favorite, an elegant blue macaw. These birds were tame and under her direction would perch on the arm or chair of group members. The conversation flowed easily when pets visited the group.

Outcomes: Caring for pets brings back memories of childhood and families. The feel of patting a live animal who returns enthusiasm gives a small, yet meaningful feeling of caregiving that elders so often miss.

Equipment list: Calm, people-loving pets such as larger dogs, large birds, rabbits, and hamsters.

SENSORY ACTIVITY: SEASHORE SENSATIONS

Goals: Various elements common to a seashore are used to distinguish textures.

Process: The leader sets the mood with a verse or short reading about going to the seashore. Prompt members to identify common seashore items that are mentioned within the introduction (reread slowly if needed). Then invite members to touch and identify these items from the tub displays. Create a tub with a built-up sandy beach area, small shells, and water reaching the beach. One or two other tubs are all sand with shells buried so that each member can find several shells. Then take the shells to a washing area. In the background, play instrumental music with seashore sounds. Encourage members to talk about past experiences at the beach.

Outcomes: The sand, water, and shells are typical of the seashore and easy to bring inside for an armchair visit. The differing textures, shapes, and activities often keep a group so involved that they are reluctant to leave. Integrating the sounds of the sea with cassette tapes enriches the experience.

Equipment list: Marker board. Several large buckets or plastic wash-tubs for creating mini-seashore and beach areas. Shells (purchased or well cleaned if natural). Sand. Small scoops. Cleanup supplies. Cassette tapes of instrumental music with seashore sounds. Short reading or verse about the seashore.

SENSORY ACTIVITY: SMOOTH OR ROUGH

Goals: Group members identify familiar objects that are smooth or coarse, then discuss how each is used.

Process: The leader gives each member a different object to hold and examine during the introduction. Going around the group, the leader asks each person if his or her object is smooth or rough. The leader and the group ask questions about the characteristics of each object that suggest whether it is smooth or rough. After everyone has a turn, the leader takes an object, describes its texture, and talks about phrases that give sensory information. Some commonly used sensory-oriented phrases are "rough as a cob," "going against the grain," "smooth as silk," and "slick as glass."

Outcomes: Distinguishing textures is suitable for all functioning groups. Some elders are highly sensitive to rough textures (even scratchy clothing labels), so be alert that the rough objects are handled carefully. Textures are often keys to reminiscences.

Equipment list: Collection of objects that are smooth (satin, velvet, feathers, soft fur) and coarse (sandpaper, corduroy, bark, pinecone).

Chapter 7

Music and Movement

Music produces a kind of pleasure which human nature cannot do without.
—Confucius, *The Book of Rites* (ca. 500 B.C.)

From the sounds of the first primitive instrument to those of a keyboard synthesizer, music styles change but music itself never goes out of style. A familiar example of the therapeutic aspect of music is found throughout the Psalms in the Bible. David perfected his performance skills playing a lyre or harp to the sheep as a shepherd boy. Later, in composing the lyrics that we know as the Psalms, the boy who became a king expressed intense emotions of joy, pleasure, fear, and depression in his music. For David, music was a calming influence, a mood enhancer, and a reflection of life. He may have been one of the first music therapists.

The notion of music as a therapeutic modality was initially recognized in academia by Michigan State University. In 1944, the university began a training program for music therapists. So much has this field grown that 40 years later there are 63 college and university programs for training music therapists recognized by the National Association for Music Therapy.

MUSIC AND MOODS

The tone, tempo, instruments, and arrangement of music are combined to evoke certain mental and physical responses from the listener. Funeral music isn't played to a polka beat. "Happy Birthday" isn't sung like the blues. The emotional content of the music is underscored by its sound. In addition, there is a physical response to music: toe tapping, hand clapping, or moving with the beat. The crisp notes of marching music correspond with the patterned steps. A waltz or lullaby elicits a smooth, gentle, floating movement. In planning music as a group modality, pay attention to the elements of the music along with the expected mental and physical responses.

Music makes connections with the senses and memories in ways that words fail, particularly for cognitively impaired or highly anxious patients. Soft, easy-paced music, including contemporary instrumentals and light classics, are an excellent background for beginning a group of restless and agitated patients. Instrumental music with nature sounds as background also provides a calming influence. Hanser (1988) reviewed various studies that demonstrated the power of music to reduce psychological and physiological reactions to stress. Merely playing cheerful or faster paced music as a means to brighten affect is a fallacy frequently doomed to elicit the opposite result.

In the same way that depressed or anxious patients can join their feelings in bibliotherapy with those of fictional characters, music can be used to focus, process, and express deep feelings. Elder groups need not avoid plaintive, blues-type music. Rather, it is to be used with proper preparation and processing within the group.

FUNCTIONS OF MUSIC IN ELDER GROUPS

Music creates an affective, pleasurable response and stimulates a cognitive response. The nature of these responses is linked to the listener's mental abilities. Higher functioning groups generally enjoy an approach to music and movement that is a mixture of affective and cognitive processing. Lower functioning groups are more comfortable working with one process at a time, predominantly affective and reminiscence. Regardless of cognitive levels, music as a modality has six primary functions in elder groups:

1   Listening: The obvious advantage is personal enjoyment for the listener. In addition, music attracts nonverbal and shy persons into the group.

2   Discussion: Impressions of music are individual and neither right nor wrong. Sharing opinions about music and its message is a nonthreatening topic. Using music that is highly identified with life stages the group has experienced results in many spin-offs for discussion from the music and lyrics.

3   Identification: Group members can relate well to music both by the mood and by the lyrical message. For example, a person who diminishes his or her own feelings hears a melancholy song and realizes that this is a more valid representation of his or her emotional condition than a false smile.

4   Reminiscence: Music is associated with many significant life events. There is the song claimed by a dating couple as "our song" and remembered for generations. Elders remain as tuned to the pop music of their youth (Frank Sinatra, Irving Berlin, and big band singers) as today's teens are to contemporary rock stars. Music is an effective modality alone or in support of reminiscence, spirituality, sensory stimulation, recreational therapy, art, and other modalities.

5   Sensation: As a sensory experience, music is satisfying to the musician and the listener. The musician is not the only one with a hands-on option. Listeners get into the act with hand clapping, foot tapping, head bobbing, finger snapping, and shoulders swaying. Sitting close to an orchestra is the best way to feel the sound vibrations. However, using relaxation techniques, groups can simulate the experience of a live concert by visualizing the sights, sounds, and energy of the recorded music.

6 Action: Experiencing the sensations is part of the action in music appreciation. Whatever the physical capabilities of the elder group, a simple movement exercise can be designed to make the most of a natural inclination to move with the music.

PLANNING THE MOVEMENTS

Group leaders need to consult with the treatment team or physician to determine the suitability of the movement exercises for each group member. A separate approval and release form that explains the activity may be signed by the elder or the elder's guardian, trustee, or health care surrogate. Smart leaders also consult with an exercise physiologist or recreational therapist for suggestions on incorporating movement for various levels of physical and cognitive conditions.

Whether using simple hand or head movements for physically limited persons or full body motion, the concept of music and movement as a combined therapeutic modality is used increasingly for elders as well as persons of other ages. Some type of regular exercise leads to psychosocial and physiological improvement for elders (Burlew, Jones, & Emerson, 1991; Sonstroem & Morgan, 1989; Viney, Benjamin, & Preston, 1988).

The movement segments are usually short and interspersed with a resting period for listening or discussion. The purpose is not to work up a sweat but rather to gradually engage a range of motion, posture (standing and sitting), and passive stretching. The music is a hook to gain attention and participation. Elders tend to be resistant and full of excuses for avoiding exercise, as are many adults. Emphasizing the music and socialization aspects of this group overcomes much of that resistance. The leader constantly reassures group members by working with realistic goals, verifying the suitability of activity to each member, arranging a comfortable environment, and giving opportunities for in-group socialization as well as acknowledging efforts (Burlew et al., 1991; Stoedefalke, 1985).

Disagreement exists among therapists on whether to segregate wheelchair patients from or integrate them with ambulatory patients. Burnside and Schmidt (1994) advocated for separation, whereas the GSE program prefers to keep members within their regular groups regardless of physical limitations. GSE leaders feel that to remove and isolate wheelchair members is emotional discrimination and a threat to group cohesiveness. When necessary during the activity, the leader gives alternate movements for those who are physically limited the same way responsible aerobics instructors show both high-impact and low-impact alternatives to their spandex-clad classes. More agile members or volunteers can become the partners of wheelchair patients, helping with arms movements or gently guiding lifeless feet in tapping to the music. Working together so that everyone participates at some level is an important element in developing group cohesion and appreciation for each other. The caring and touch given one elder by another can be the most therapeutic aspect of this or any group modality.

MUSIC AND MOVEMENT: BIG BAND

Goals: Swing music gets feet tapping and arms moving for physical and mood enhancement.

Process: As the group enters, play a peppy big band song to set the tone. Members are seated in straight-back chairs with space between for arm movement. This is also suitable for wheelchair patients with some assistance. The leader introduces the songs, then suggests and displays simple movements with the music. Arm circles, head nodding, hand clapping, simulated drumming, feet tapping, rocking the body side to side, and stepping forward and then back are gentle moves that many ambulatory persons can perform to music. Assist patients in wheelchairs or with limited mobility by offering to carefully guide arms or feet in time to the music. If possible, invite the facility's physical therapist or a community recreation leader for elder activities to direct the movement.

Outcomes: Moving to familiar music is pleasurable and provides some exercise.

Equipment list: Audio equipment and records or tapes of big band music. Chairs.

MUSIC AND MOVEMENT: WORLD WAR II MUSIC

Goals: Music and memories of a place, time, and significant event are linked. In this global war effort, music was an important coping mechanism that can be an encouragement in present difficulties.

Process: The leader brings an anthology of World War II music recorded on cassette tape or in sheet music if a piano or portable keyboard is available. If possible, arrange the music in chronological order. Play a song, then ask members to recall when they first heard the song, what was happening in their lives, and how meaningful this song was in coping with their emotions during that time. Invite musically talented members to play the melodies while the group joins in singing or humming. With higher functioning groups, give copies of the lyrics to encourage singing along.

Outcomes: These musical memories track the nation's response to war and victory in a period that personally affected elders and their loved ones. Identify the music and the messages that gave them strength and how they still use those coping skills.

Equipment list: Recordings, sheet music, and books of World War II songs. Cassette tape player and music tapes. Piano or keyboard.

MUSIC AND MOVEMENT: MARCHING

Goals: Parade tunes and military marches are background for movement activity.

Process: Play crisp parade march as group members enter. The leader reads a brief comment about parades or shows photos of major parades such as Fourth of July parades or the Thanksgiving Day Parade in New York City. Talk briefly about memories of watching or participating in parades. Spend at least half the session doing marching movements to well-known music. The leader acts as drum major, directing the group to march in place, wave, swing arms, and march around the room to music. Wheelchair patients join the parade with an assistant pushing the chair. Choose music that is energetic enough to get feet tapping without overexertion.

Outcomes: Invigorating for body and mind. The parade–movement connection is a natural for encouraging participation among physically able persons.

Equipment list: Recordings, sheet music, and books of parade and march music. Piano or keyboard. Drums and homemade cymbals.

MUSIC AND MOVEMENT: PATRIOTIC

Goals: Involve several senses through stirring patriotic songs.

Process: A slower patriotic song plays as members gather. Members take their seats in chairs arranged with movement space between. The leader displays the flag and invites members to rise or, if in a wheelchair, show attention and join in singing the national anthem. If there are group members from other nations, make an effort to get a recording of their national anthem as well. After returning to seats, members are given kazoos or cymbals as their instruments to play in time with the music. Play a song and prompt members to play their instruments and sing if they choose. As a break between songs, let members comment on personal meanings they ascribe to the patriotic music. This activity can be done as part of a music series or saved for patriotic holidays.

Outcomes: Hearing, singing, humming, and hands-on instruments offers several methods of sensory involvement in this music and movement activity. Even lower functioning groups participate well in this exercise.

Equipment list: Recordings, sheet music, and books of patriotic music. Piano or keyboard. Kazoos or homemade cymbals for each participant. U.S. flag.

MUSIC AND MOVEMENT: NATURE SOUNDS

Goals: Relating musical imagery with sights and sounds of nature.

Process: The leader introduces the exercise as a way to see with the ears and imagine being in a forest or on a beach through the music. If the leader is trained in guided imagery, the experience becomes even richer for participants. With imagery, this musical nature exploration also becomes a relaxation exercise. If not used with guided imagery, play part of the tape while everyone listens. Then replay the tape and ask for members to speak out and identify a nature sound. Encourage members to describe the image they get from listening to the music. After discussing the nature sounds on the tape, play a final time.

Outcomes: Through this type of music, a group with limited mobility can travel in their imaginations to places out of their reach. Memories of travel and childhood experiences emerge. Lower functioning groups respond very well to this exercise.

Equipment list: Tapes of music with nature sounds such as rain, waves, wind, birds, or storms.

MUSIC AND MOVEMENT: SING-ALONG SONGS

Goals: Recapture the enjoyment of a family activity popular before television, singing around the piano.

Process: Before the group's arrival, arrange chairs in a semicircle around the piano. At each chair, place pages with lyrics typed in large print. The leader and a volunteer serve as director and musician. Warm up with a few easy songs. Invite members to share a memory about family or neighborhood sing-alongs. Continue with songs, varying the tempo and ending with upbeat, positive songs.

Outcomes: Recreating a pleasurable time and singing familiar tunes is a comforting, nostalgic activity.

Equipment list: Piano or keyboard. Copies of song lyrics in large type.

MUSIC AND MOVEMENT: TRIP TO HAWAII

Goals: Music from the tropics encourages fluid movements and senses of the exotic.

Process: Surround the group room with colorful streamers, artificial flowers, and tropical posters. The leader or a guest instructor explains the activity of enjoying Hawaiian music while performing a chairside hula. Each person gets an paper lei and two streamers. Using a videotape as a guide or copying movements from a book on hula, the leader demonstrates some basic movements, waving the streamers. If you don't know actual hula hand movements, make them up as you go. Play a song and give suggestions for movements. As the group gets more involved, play a hula song with lyrics and instruct them to use any movement desired to communicate the message. Anyone who prefers to may stand and sway carefully with the music. Patients in wheelchairs and those less steady on their feet remain seated. With lower functioning groups, the leader can get them moving, then go around to each person and encourage or guide them to move with the music. If the facility will allow, serve punch and finger-food-sized tropical fruit bites to complete the island experience.

Outcomes: Tropical music motivates listeners to move and sway easily in keeping with the rhythm. Group members will also recall many of the Hawaiian songs as part of their musical memories.

Equipment list: Hawaiian music, both instrumental and vocal. Cassette player. Optional video of dancers performing hula, videocassette player, and television. Colorful paper leis and artificial orchids. Borrow tropical posters from a travel agent. Streamers of crepe paper or ribbon approximately 1 yard each (two per person). Bite-sized pieces of tropical fruit.

MUSIC AND MOVEMENT: OUTDOOR CONCERT

Goals: Simulate an outdoor concert with recorded music in a comfortable outdoor setting.

Process: Before group, the leader arranges for sturdy outdoor chairs to be placed on the facility patio or adjacent yard. Clear a safe walking and wheelchair path. Bring a portable tape player with speakers. If possible, bring coffee or lemonade and snack foods to enjoy during the concert. When the group is seated, the leader introduces the music and tells something about it. Good choices for this activity are Broadway show tunes or light classical music. Another wonderful option is to have a local high school musical ensemble perform a live concert.

Outcomes: Enjoying music outdoors is reminiscent of town square bands performing on summer afternoons. A casual atmosphere and fresh air enhance music appreciation for groups of all function levels.

Equipment list: Tape player with speakers. Recorded music or live performers. Coffee or lemonade and snack foods.

MUSIC AND MOVEMENT: KITCHEN BAND

Goals: The pleasure is doubled by participating in making the sounds.

   Process: If the group is capable, they can have one session for making or assembling kitchen band instruments. At the performance session, the leader can bring background music on tape. Kitchen band instruments are limited only by the leader's creativity and may include spoons, pie tins, pots as drums, and other common items. If the group wants to practice, they can perform in the day room for other residents. Kitchen bands are fun for all ages and easy to do.

   Outcomes: Participation and entertainment set to music that is suitable for groups of all levels.

   Equipment list: Kitchen band instruments. Tape player and background music.

MUSIC AND MOVEMENT: HANDBELL CHORUS

Goals: Another participatory adventure in music with easy movement.

Process: The leader may borrow handbell sets from a local church or band. If not available, any kind of bells will do. The least expensive method is to use small holiday decorator bells joined by a ribbon chain. The sound is not nearly as important as the participation. With high-functioning groups using actual handbell sets, the leader can point to the person as a sign to ring the bell. Otherwise with this group or low-functioning groups, ring or shake the bells in time to music.

Outcomes: The sounds may vary, yet making music as a group is a satisfying activity for many elders.

Equipment list: Handbell sets or homemade bell chains. Recorded music.

Chapter 8

Phototherapy

The image is for us the way to the original; in it we touch at least the hem of the garment of the eternal idea.   —Odo Casel

How many words is a picture worth? Capturing a moment in time or a visual image of a feeling, pictures can stimulate a thousand words or a dozen unspoken emotions. Phototherapy is to the eyes what bibliotherapy is to the mind. The concept of phototherapy in the medical realm is linked with using different light spectrums to treat sunlight-deprived persons for such maladies as seasonal affective disorder. The GSE modality, phototherapy, is intended to cast light in a metaphorical manner. In this modality, phototherapy is a psychological process that uses photos to deal with emotional symptoms or to facilitate growth and change (Stewart, 1979).

Phototherapy is an emerging specialty with many connections to art therapy. Yet the stark reality that is captured on film is less dependent on interpretation than many types of art. Photos can be lovely, shimmering, and richly colorful or no-frills black-and-whites from the morning newspaper. Sufficient variety of technique and creativity exists to pair with an appropriate therapeutic application.

Family photo albums as well as unrelated photos of others can be used with elder groups to encourage communication, process feelings at safe distance, and recall memories. These snapshots (a remarkably descriptive term) are literally flashes capturing moments in time. Photos show things as they are compared with memories that recall things with or without personal interpretation. Colors in a photo come from impressions on the film as interpreted at the processing lab. Emotions, beliefs, thoughts, background, and other abstract elements are impressions that color memories in very individual and stylized ways. Experience this difference by finding an old photo of a family event. Ask two or three other people who were in the photo (or present at the event) to tell the story of what happened. The reports may have as little in common as agreeing that dinner was held at Grandma's house. Beyond that, the actual images are personalized by being "filtered" through each person's beliefs, feelings, and attitudes. Memories as snapshots of the mind are often not as clear or as accurate as snapshots taken with a nonemotional camera.

Leaders need to be aware that elders from some cultural backgrounds are resistant to working with photos as they are too personal or an invasion of private space. Such attitudes may be related to historical views by some American Indian and African groups who feel that having a photo taken compromises their spiritual being. Elders of various cultural heritages are likely to respond adversely to photos depicting violence, interpersonal conflict, or destruction. The harsh realism of today's typical news photos are both disturbing and threatening to persons who grew up in an era where photos were simple, less available, and treasured possessions.

HOW TO USE PHOTOS IN GROUP

Phototherapy with elders is less concerned with checking on the absolute truth of memories than with using the images to clarify and enrich memories with emotional, sensory, and relationship details. As a very affective modality, the amount of photo stimulus is carefully monitored to avoid overwhelming elders. Photos of self or family offer a low-key means of examining false beliefs (i.e., "always the ugly duckling" or "never spent time with my children"). Photos of personally significant events (graduation, marriage, birthdays, holidays) stimulate reminiscence and a sense of belonging.

When photos of the group members are not available, substitute photos of unrelated others that represent comparable times, events, or life stages. Magazines are full of colorful pictorial advertisements. Leaders interested in the modality need to keep adding to a collection of old photos gathered from family and friends. Another great way to add to the collection is by buying old photo albums at garage sales and thrift stores where a few dollars can purchase a full album or box of old photos. The local historical society is another source of copies of photos or borrowed slide shows.

NONIDENTIFIED PHOTOS

The nonidentified photos can be as effective as those that are identified. A photo of a young 1940s Army nurse may receive such varied reactions as "She reminds me of my sister who left home to join the nurses corps," "she's the cheerful nurse who cared for me at the VA hospital," or "she's like so many brave young women who did their part for the war effort." This is more than a game of "let's pretend." It's an exercise in expanding on what is seen in the picture with what the image means to the observer. Particularly with cognitively impaired groups, there is a greater freedom to draw assumptions about the nonidentified person's name, age, lifestyle, and personality. There is also less frustration or pressure to recognize people who are vaguely familiar as is often true with photos of family or older peers.

Phototherapy also works well with nonverbal and verbally limited elders. Simple photos with clear, distinct facial expressions can be used to inquire about feelings or mood. The leader may present two or three (but no more) choices showing a same-sex person who is smiling, pensive, or sad, then ask the elder to point to the one that "feels like you feel today." A variation on this is for the leader to look at several photos with the elder and observe those photos to which he or she is attracted. A more structured activity, the photo collage, allows both verbal and nonverbal elders to make a visual statement that represents feelings, emotions, or life experiences (Katz, 1987).

PHOTOTHERAPY: TELL A PICTURE STORY—MAGAZINES

Goals: The picture is a springboard for reminiscence or expression of feelings.

Process: The leader opens with comments on how every picture tells a story without words. Using a color ad or photo, the leader displays it and gives his or her own impressions of the story behind it. Then each group member is given a different color picture to study. Going around the group, each person shows the picture and tells the picture story as she or he sees it. The leader may ask less verbal persons questions to help them focus on the picture story. A newer group or a low-functioning group may work from the same picture. Together, each member can contribute observations that the leader summarizes on a marker board to tell the picture story. The best pictures for this activity are those with a single action and easy-to-recognize objects. The pictures that elicit the most detailed or personalized responses in GSE groups are those with one or two children playing, a family in the home, a tranquil garden, or babies.

Outcomes: Elders at all levels of functioning can become involved in this interpretative, projective activity. Many responses are general and evident from the pictures. Other members, particularly cognitively impaired persons, are prompted by the pictures to personalize responses and reveal vivid experiences or feelings.

Equipment list: Cut out large color advertisements or photos from magazines and paste each on sturdy cardboard. Marker board and boldly colored markers.

PHOTOTHERAPY: TELL A PICTURE STORY—FAMILY ALBUM

Goals: Pictures of self and family are part of reminiscences and reality checks.

Process: Before group or at the first session of a series, the leader explains how familiar photos will be the center of this activity and asks each person to bring personal photos or albums. If possible, have each person bring at least one photo of him- or herself as a small child, teenager, young adult, or older adult. Another theme for this group is magic moments such as family holidays, graduation, marriage, birth or adoption of a child, and activities with friends. With higher functioning groups, have each member describe him- or herself at specific ages or stages before showing the photos. In GSE groups, a woman who claimed to never have been included in family events was seen in several photos looking content amid relatives. Another man who said that his son never spent time with him is seen in photos of the two of them fishing, bowling, and rebuilding a boat. Through photos, one can confront myths or false beliefs about the individual's relationship to family and friends. On the positive side, photos affirm connections between generations, siblings, and friends as well as show continuity. Lower functioning groups manage well with reminiscences and feelings evoked from photos, yet are less likely to develop new insights.

Outcomes: Personal photos are a pictorial history that are sometimes more accurate than memories and family legends. These photos become vehicles for closure, resolution, and affirmation.

Equipment list: Family photos of each member. It's best to use larger photos or enlarge their size on a photocopier.

PHOTOTHERAPY: AUTOBIOGRAPHICAL PHOTO COLLAGE

Goals: This activity gives a visual introduction over the life span.

Process: This exercise requires two or three sessions and some additional volunteer assistance for group members. Several weeks before beginning, ask members to locate five to seven photos of themselves at various ages and with important people from their past and present. Or get approval to send a letter to each member's family requesting photos. Also obtain approval from the facility to hang the finished collage on or outside the door to each person's room. The leader introduces the project and briefly outlines the steps to completion. Writing the steps in large print on poster board is a helpful reference. The leader can go around the table and work with each person separately or involve the group in reviewing everyone's photos. Assist with trimming photos for fit and balance. The leader can take a quick-developing photo of each member as the centerpiece of the collage. Around the perimeter, other photos are arranged. The member prints a caption on plain paper and glues it below the collage. This allows for errors. Or an assistant can write the caption as dictated by the individual. If the group can work and converse, talk about recollections from the photos and relationships with other people in those pictures. Lower functioning members and those with limited vision will need more assistance and a slower pace. When the collage is finished, insert it in a frame and ask each member to present and describe his or her autobiographical collage.

Outcomes: As a mini photo history, this collage is a source of pleasure and identity reaffirmation to each person daily as well as a way for staff to relate better to residents. Any time the collage is complimented by visitors, the resident feels pride in having completed the project.

Equipment list: Plain posterboard cut to fit inside a 8 × 10 or 11 × 17 clear plastic, nonbreakable frame. Safety scissors. Precut construction paper borders. Colorful stickers. Paper on which to write captions. Glue or photo-mounting corners. Camera with quick-developing film.

PHOTOTHERAPY: AMERICAN LIFE PHOTO ESSAYS

Goals: Looking at people and places that are part of the American scene that are similar to and different than an individual's experiences.

Process: The leader may open with a Walt Whitman verse or other words that focus on Americana. Ask each group member to name the state or region in which they grew up or where they lived most of their life. Point out the areas on a U.S. map. Then begin to explore the pictures in a photo essay book. Focus on themes, ages, people, places, or activities. As in the "tell a picture story" activities, have each member comment on the story behind the photo. Then read the caption or explanation from the book. Encourage group members to share memories of similar scenes from the past or present experiences.

Outcomes: Great photos are compelling and mentally stimulating. Responses may be directed toward the actual photo content or the memory accessed because of the photo.

Equipment list: Coffee-table-sized color photo books from the library or similar photos on color slides. If using slides, get a slide projector and large screen. A national map.

PHOTOTHERAPY: A FEELING COLLAGE

Goals: Using photos of nonidentified persons and places to display a range of feelings.

Process: The leader begins by showing some very emotive photos and seeking the group's response on what they feel when viewing each photo. Choose some very clear images such as the famous victory kiss of a sailor and a nurse at the close of World War II. Give a set of pictures to each group member to review. Instruct them to keep any photos that show an emotion they recently felt (or currently feel). Collect the discards and distribute to other group members. Allow one or two sessions to review and choose emotive photos. When every member has at least five photos, distribute poster board. Depending on their dexterity, members can trim photos themselves or with assistance. Arrange photos on the board in any order desired. Members can write feeling words on the poster board or glue on preprinted words. The leader gets, ahead of time, copies of large-type emotive words (i.e., love, anger, sad, happy, or confused) with an ample supply for participants. Be very nondirective in each person's choice of photos. One person will have all happy photos, and another will choose tense scenes. Invite (but don't require) each person to talk about the collage and its meaning. Display the completed collages in the community room.

Outcomes: Emotional responses to photos can be safer to express than verbal admissions. Cognitively impaired persons are occasionally better able to reveal themselves by the visual–emotional connection than with a verbal–emotional response.

Equipment list: Old magazines, catalogs, or news photos. Safety scissors. Posterboard. Glue.

PHOTOTHERAPY: FACES OF CHILDREN

Goals: Recall the wonders of childhood and parental feelings of sharing those moments of discovery.

Process: The leader tells a brief story or reads an essay with very vivid descriptions of a childhood event and emotional responses. The group is asked to consider how much of a child's feelings are evident in facial expressions. Then each member is given a picture involving a child. After a pause to study the pictures, group members present their photos and tell about the action and emotion shown. With each presentation, the leader asks if anyone can share a time that they saw a child in such a situation. How much of the child's feelings do they understand? What would they like to say to the child?

Outcomes: Elders are frequently removed from children and enjoy even a photo glimpse of their playful, forthright behaviors. Acting as the child's advocate, some elders will connect with feelings and unresolved issues of their inner child, which is more distantly projected onto the photo.

Equipment list: Pictures of children of various ages and ethnicity and with various facial expressions. May also use the therapeutic poster of children's emotions. Brief story or essay about a childhood event.

PHOTOTHERAPY: TRAVEL BY PHOTO

Goals: Armchair travel is without physical or financial limitations, yet brings exotic places within reach of the imagination.

Process: Before group, the leader collects colorful photos and related objects and packs them in a suitcase to be unpacked at group. It may be possible to borrow a slide show or video from a local travel agent or auto club. You may also get an experienced commentator along with the show. Another option is to videotape a TV or cable travel show or documentary. Arrange chairs in rows as on an airplane or in a v-wing configuration so everyone gets a good view. As the group gathers, distribute the homemade passports which have a list of several locations. For higher functioning groups, the leader gives several clues about today's travel itinerary. Then for all groups, name the location and point to it on a map or globe before beginning the presentation. For lower functioning groups, interrupt the show approximately every 10 minutes and discuss what was seen. This compensates for short attention spans. Even with higher functioning groups, avoid videos exceeding 25–30 minutes. Allow time to discuss what was seen and anything new learned from this armchair trip. Then the leader stamps and dates the passport and tells of plans to see one of the other locations listed.

Outcomes: Travel is said to broaden a person's horizons. In this group, armchair travel allows members to journey in their imaginations to places they are not likely to go or recall places they have previously been. Focusing on the differences in colors, sights, textures, people, buildings, and tourist attractions is both entertaining and informative.

Equipment list: Travel posters, brochures, and books. Photos and related objects packed in a suitcase. Map or globe. Slides or video presentation. A homemade passport or postcard souvenir. A date stamp or symbol stamp (available in stationery stores and children's toy stores).

PHOTOTHERAPY: HOLIDAY IMAGES

Goals: Present a more vibrant view of the holiday and differing methods of celebration.

Process: Christmas, Thanksgiving, New Year's, Valentine's Day, Memorial Day, and Fourth of July are excellent subjects for this phototherapy activity. A few weeks before the stated holiday or during the week of the holiday, the group views photos of celebrations and discusses the scenes. The leader may show photos of past and present events, similar holidays around the world, or children at holidays as focal point for the discussion. GSE leaders were surprised that a high-functioning group wanted to discuss how they celebrated Christmas during World War II. After searching the library, photo essay books were located with scenes of both battlefields and family back home. Rather than being depressed by the subject, the group radiated in sharing how their feelings of hope transcended the circumstances. From that reminiscence came a renewed spirit of refusing to be limited by things outside the self. The therapeutic implications of this session for coping with present problems was far beyond anything GSE leaders planned. Don't be afraid to mix photos of various emotions and situations in holiday scenes.

Outcomes: Holidays are packed with nostalgia and recurrent feelings of loss as well as happiness and excitement. With minimal involvement in holiday plans, some elders choose to emotionally disengage. Allowing expression of positive and negative feelings, group members can find new meanings for holidays and ideally create a family and a celebration among themselves.

Equipment list: Photos or slides of holiday activities, food, clothing, and people engaged in traditional holiday activities. Recycled holiday card photos.

PHOTOTHERAPY: MATURE IMAGES

Goals: Challenge negative views of aging that are ingrained by our youth-centered society.

Process: The leader begins by asking members to give their definitions of attractiveness for men and women. What characteristics show dignity, strength, and pride? Show a series of photos of older men and women either in prints or on slides. Then show the series again, stopping to discuss characteristics of each photo. The leader writes the descriptions on the marker board in a positive column or a negative column. Positive descriptions are timeless (e.g., lovely, distinguished, confident). Negative descriptions are often age-defaming (e.g., tired, wrinkled, stooped). Return to the photos that were described negatively. Encourage the group to find another, positive way to describe the image. The "tired" face can also be "dedicated to helping others." The leader can also present photos of senior adult magazine models. Ask the group to debate whether elder models are attractive because of their age or because they look younger.

Outcomes: If teenagers seek every mirror, elders shun them. Learning to see beauty in the aging body is a means of acceptance that can increase participation in self-care.

Equipment list: Photos, slides, or photo essay books featuring older men and women of various ages, socioeconomic status, health, mobility, and emotional expressions. Marker board.

PHOTOTHERAPY: NEWS IMAGES

Goals: Looking at current events through the photographer's eyes.

Process: This is another way to bring current events into the overall group agenda. The leader scans news sources for major stories and human interest stories accompanied by photos. Begin by inquiring about any major or breaking news event such as a hurricane, earthquake, congressional vote, or trial. Show related photos and discuss how effectively the story is portrayed in the pictures. Then present the less-promoted human interest stories (e.g., a fire rescue, three generations graduate together, or a new community theater company). Without revealing the headline or the text, ask members what they think the story is about from looking at the picture. After a few guesses, read the text. Members can comment on how well or how poorly the picture tells the story.

Outcomes: In this activity, members gain information and use analytical skills.

Equipment list: Larger news photos from newspapers or magazines mounted on poster board with the story pasted on the back side.

Chapter 9

Humor

There are no things by which the troubles and difficulties of this life can be resisted better than with wit and humor.

—H. W. Beecher

Laughter is a medicine too often overlooked in geriatric treatment. Leaders and students who are new to geriatric work are inclined to make the mistaken assumption that humor is not appreciated in a nursing home or retirement community. Such an assumption is another manifestation of therapeutic prejudice. If we applaud the efforts of entertainers and staff to bring laughter to terminally ill children and young adults in a cancer ward, why do we deny the healing potential of humor for elderly persons? Clearly we are not laughing at the plight of age, illness, or immobility any more than we are laughing at the ravages of cancer. What we are doing is providing an alternative focus by encouraging elders to laugh with us. Norman Cousins's (1979) *Anatomy of an Illness* makes a strong case for humor even in dire situations on the basis of his use of laughter as part of his healing experience. Understanding this principle is the key to appreciating humor as a geriatric group modality.

Despite pain and physical problems, GSE groups use a variety of techniques that connect to the humor sources of and memories from the elder's past. Mixing in humor after more intense modalities helps both the leader and the group members avoid therapy burnout. The physical and emotional release of hearty laughter can be prompted by anecdotes from magazines, videotapes of children, jokes, or asking elders to recall their favorite funny stories from their families.

EFFICACY OF HUMOR

Humor studies are no laughing matter (pardon the pun). A year-long study (McGuire, Boyo, & James, 1992) on the effectiveness of humor with 86 nursing

home residents substantiated the benefits of humor as an intervention for improving the perceived quality of life. Humor in group work functions as an anxiety
regulator (Tuttman, 1991), strengthens the treatment alliance (Schnarch, 1990),
and increases social interest (Rutherford, 1994). Ewers, Jacobson, Powers, and
McConney (1983) considered humor a necessary tonic for seniors in residential
care. Their program used a variety of activities and resources in what they called
the "humor toolbox." Joel Goodman's Humor Project teaches health care professionals how to guide patients in identifying the humor in everyday events and
applying humor in their life situations. Lederman (1988) also saw humor as a tool
for encouraging the healthy expression of pleasure. At Morton Plant Mease Hospital in Clearwater, Florida, patients of all ages are treated with intensive care
from the Comedy Cart. Like GSE and Ewers et al., the therapeutic tools of the
Comedy Cart include a multimedia spectrum of resources brought directly to
patients or groups.

Freud (1960) recognized humor as a way to continue childhood playfulness
in a form that adults could accept. Although a patient may use humor as a defense
mechanism, Kennedy (1991) found this more workable than a patient who is
humorless. Satow (1991) suggested that looking beyond the psychoanalytic and
object relations explanations of humor is to discover the self-psychology view in
which laughter has adaptive and mastery aspects within a group.

The leader who is comfortable with humor is likely to best use this modality.
You don't have to be a comedian or a performer, merely a person who enjoys a
hearty laugh and desires to share that pleasure with others. The most effective
humor for geriatric groups is universal, appropriate, and respectful, not sarcastic
or political. Some groups are more willing to personalize humor, and others prefer to keep it at a distance.

LAUGHTER

Laughing together is a type of bonding for groups and their leader. Dimmer, Carroll, and Wyatt (1990) reviewed the literature and research on humor and con-
cluded that sharing humor creates a closeness and equality between therapist and
client. Lusterman (1992) suggested that humor strengthens the therapeutic
alliance. Finally, humor simply feels good. Peter and Dana (1982) found that as a
patient focuses more on pain, the pain increases. Introduce laughter and the
patient's attention is diverted from focusing on pain while endorphins are
released into the brain as a natural mood enhancer. Therapeutically applied,
humor becomes a stabilizing force for body chemistry and organ functions
(MacHovec, 1991).

Humor begets humor. Often the best outcome is to let it happen and allow
group members to rediscover how laughter brings joy to the moment regardless
of their present circumstances.

HUMOR: CLASSIC RADIO COMEDY

Goals: Return to those laughing days of yesteryear and enjoy them anew.

Process: The leader begins by asking group members to recall their favorite comedy on radio. Who was the star and what kind of situations were typical? Because radio was such a significant family entertainment source, many elders have vivid memories of gathering in the evening to listen to regular programs. After a brief discussion, the leader plays a portion from an old radio show. Another way of using this material is to play short segments from several shows and make a contest of identifying the names of characters and shows. With low-functioning groups, use only short segments and identify the characters.

Outcomes: Not a sound was wasted in creating word pictures for the radio comedy audience. Thus, these programs appeal to the senses and the imagination in ways that television cannot duplicate. The involvement and entertainment are suitable for persons at all levels of functioning.

Equipment list: Cassette tapes of old radio shows and portable cassette player. Test volume to determine if extra speakers are needed in the group room.

HUMOR: CLASSIC TELEVISION COMEDY

Goals: Similar to radio comedy, this is for enjoyment with more visuals to support the humor.

Process: As with old radio shows, the leader asks the group to recall their favorite television comedies and characters. Display the videotape of classic TV shows and briefly talk about how easy it is to record and replay with today's technology. Ask members to share their first experiences with a television set and how it compared with radio. Play a short introductory scene to be certain everyone can hear and see well. Make adjustments before beginning the tape. Use a library tape or record the show, skipping commercials to reduce time and maintain the program's continuity. If time permits, discuss the most humorous scenes and what caused each person to laugh at this show or character.

Outcomes: Television best captures nonverbal humor with body motions and facial expressions. This is another means of provoking laughter and a temporary escape into a less serious environment.

Equipment list: Videotape player, videotape of classic TV comedy, and large-screen television.

HUMOR: SHARING JOKES

Goals: Exercise spontaneous humor.

Process: The leader can open group with a brief comment on the history of jokes or launch right into reading jokes. At any time, group members are welcome to interject a joke they recall. Appropriate limits may be set, such as no foul language and nothing that demeans a race, gender, religious, or ethnic group. A method to get others involved is to copy jokes in large print, with each joke on two cards: the opening part on one card and the punch line on the other. Color code the cards. After the blue-card reader gives the opening part, the other blue-card reader completes the joke.

Outcomes: Demonstrates how laughter is another kind of "medicine" for groups.

Equipment list: Joke books from bookstore or library. Clip and save jokes from *Reader's Digest* and other magazines. Color-coded cards with jokes in large print.

HUMOR: MATURE HUMOR

Goals: Finding humor in aspects of aging.

Process: Introducing this topic, the leader shares a funny situation in which she or he was involved. This group gives space to laugh at personal frustrations by laughing with others. The leader shows a series of mature humor cartoons or reads jokes and a few brief stories. Members are encouraged to interject at any time their humorous experiences since moving to the facility (if residential) or in the past year (for community elders).

Outcomes: There are so many serious aspects to aging (pain, limited mobility, and memory loss) that the ability to laugh at ourselves and our frustrations is a positive coping strategy.

Equipment list: Book of jokes or essays with a humorous look at senior adult life. Cartoons or articles from senior magazines such as *Modern Maturity.* A GSE favorite is *A Treasury of Senior Humor* by James E. Myers.

HUMOR: ESSAYS

Goals: Finding humor is the commonplace.

Process: The leader selects a series of humorous essays that deal with ordinary aspects of life. An alternative is to choose several essays from different authors on a single subject, such as waiting in the doctor's office or struggling with childproof medicine bottle caps. Talk about what elements of the situation are funny and share any similar experiences. Does the author convey humor with unusual words, dialogue, or convoluted situations? With several essays on a single subject, discuss how each author used a different style to create humor.

Outcomes: Finding humor in everyday life reminds members of the many possibilities for laughter no matter what the circumstances are.

Equipment list: Library books of well-known humorists such as Bennett Cerf, Erma Bombeck, and Dave Barry. Essays found in magazines or newspapers.

HUMOR: INNOCENT HUMOR OF CHILDREN

Goals: Reexperiencing humor through children's viewpoints.

Process: Presenting children's humor can be done with photos, videotapes, or reading. Even videotapes of the preschool play, a children's parade, or young children telling knock-knock jokes are ideal for this group. The leader can also read from a children's joke book. Many of those jokes seem timeless. You will be surprised at how many jokes have been passed down through several generations of children.

Outcomes: Enjoying laughing with children and recalling humor from childhood experiences.

Equipment list: Books such as *Kids Say the Darndest Things* by Art Linkletter. Videotapes of children, videocassette player, and large-screen television.

HUMOR: JESTERS OF OUR LIVES

Goals: Remembering the people who brought laughter to us.

Process: The leader shows a photo of the court jester and speaks about this character's role as a medieval comedian. Give group members a few moments to think of the person or persons who always know how to bring laughter and levity to them. Who are the jesters they have known? What was special about those persons? What was their style of humor? Can they recall their favorite jokes or comic actions?

Outcomes: Learning to recall the people from our lives who shared humor with us.

Equipment list: Photo and article on court jesters.

HUMOR: CLOWNS

Goals: From childhood through adulthood, clowns symbolize fun that is ageless.

Process: The leader surrounds the room with clown photos and bright balloons for a party atmosphere. If possible, invite several local clowns to assist with group. Begin by introducing the visiting clowns or showing videos of clowns. Set up a face-painting station for any group members who want to participate. Start a discussion about the first experience with clowns and how they appear through a child's eyes. Allow the clowns to present a skit or engage members in a simple activity. Bring an instant developing camera and offer to take a photo of each member with the clown.

Outcomes: This activity is pure fun and offers a chance to feel like a kid at the circus again.

Equipment list: Photos or videotapes of clowns or actual clowns. Television. Balloons. Face-painting station. Camera with quick-developing film.

HUMOR: COMICS

Goals: On the comics page are laughs about all ages and stages of life, with something that appeals to everyone.

Process: The leader brings enough Sunday comics for every member. With volunteers from the group, take turns reading the comics aloud. Talk about some of the long-lasting comic strips. What makes their characters transcend several generations and remain funny? What are some older comics that are no longer printed? Would those characters and situations still be funny today?

Outcomes: The comics are good for laughs and reminiscences about how humor has changed over the years.

Equipment list: Sunday comics pages (in color). Familiar comic books.

HUMOR: FAMILY FUNNIES

Goals: This is a retrospective on family life and humorous events that are part of the family legend.

Process: The leader begins with a personal story or brief essay about a funny family situation. The group is invited to share those special stories about relatives or events that become the legends of laughter in each family.

Outcomes: Family humor is deeply personal and satisfying to recall.

Equipment list: None.

Chapter 10

Spirituality

The segregation of the spiritual life from the practical life is a curse that falls impartially upon both sides of our existence.

—Lewis Mumford

Reaching the seventh and eighth decade of life prompts most elders to contemplate their future beyond this lifetime. It's not a question of being "religious," although that is the means many choose to explore spirituality. As aging and illness remove the ability to depend totally on the self for meeting needs, there is an inherent desire to discover or strengthen that quality of self that is impervious to fleshly decline. Spirituality is that all-important quality so often ignored by caregivers and therapists.

Many professionals fear that a search for spiritual awareness is promoting a certain religious belief, mainly that of the group leader. Clearly the potential for proselytizing exists; there is no values-free counseling. Donald Grimm (1994) suggested that therapists who understand their own spiritual beliefs, respect cross-cultural differences, and remain sensitive to others are capable of dealing with a client's spiritual issues in a manner that enhances the opportunity for a positive therapeutic result. Prest and Keller (1993) challenged therapists to work with those spiritual systems of clients that provide strength and support. They further contended that the decision not to deal with spirituality often begins with therapists who fail to make a distinction between spirituality and organized religion and who assume that spiritual practices are a problem rather than a positive influence in the client's life.

SPIRITUALITY AND COPING

Elders have a strong need to clarify their own spirituality as a coping mechanism. Options for change may be minimal in the physical or mental realm. Finding or renewing a spiritual connection can be the remaining viable change that makes the latter days of life more satisfying. This search may involve a reconnection to the past or taking a new direction to find answers in the present.

Why do therapists and group leaders find excuses to ignore spiritual, basically existential, concerns among elders? Whose mortality issues are threatened in this exploration: those of the leader or those of the elders? Working with elder groups, leaders must face the fact that death will invade and reduce the group more unpredictably than any other factor. Can you as group leader cope with so much loss? Are you knowledgeable in techniques for dealing with grief and loss issues? Two of the least effective ways to deal with this (that have been observed in other programs) is to pause for 1 minute of silent prayer, then move on to the regular agenda, or to ignore the event. Both approaches produce anger and distrust in elders. As a 92-year-old woman observed, "There was plenty of concern when a nurse died in a car accident, but when one of us drops, so what? Change the sheets and move in the next person as if nothing important happened."

Each time a group member dies, the group's agenda turns to a single-session grief process. A wealth of information and training in grief groups is available through hospice. Otherwise, a geriatric group leader prepares for this task best by seeking training or coleadership experiences to learn appropriate skills for grief groups. Hughes (1995) suggested that leaders learn to balance their psychodynamic skills with the equally important subjective skills of compassion, flexibility, listening, willingness to learn, creativity, and fallibility. Also note grief groups (exercises 9 and 10) later in this chapter. Other GSE activities adaptable for grief are postcards from eternity (exercise 4), in which members compose postcards to the deceased member and a wish for a happy afterlife, and spiritual legacy (exercise 7), in which group members recall how the deceased member impressed each surviving member in ways that became lasting spiritual remembrances. An expression of spirituality, individual and sincere, is significant in coping with grief and losses that are part of aging (Reed, 1991).

SPIRITUALITY AND THERAPY

A competent, self-aware group leader who can deal with each member's spirituality in a nonjudgmental, accepting manner has a powerful therapeutic force. In spirituality are a wealth of metaphors useful for relaxation and introspection. Parables, stories of personal spiritual experiences, and reading the Bible, Torah, or books sacred to other religions support verbal expressions of beliefs. There are also nonverbal expressions that communicate a belief, such as a Catholic's making the sign of the cross or a charismatic's raising hands in praise. In addition, ascribing value to religious objects such as prayer books, rosary beads, or prayer shawls are nonverbal means of identifying with a formal spiritual belief system. GSE's group on spiritual symbols (exercise 8) allows members to share these verbal and nonverbal symbols as a way in which each individual invokes spirituality for coping.

The group leader needs to impose only one essential variation on the golden rule in allowing various expressions of spirituality: Respect the beliefs of others as you want them to respect your beliefs. Kept within that context, any verbal or nonverbal expressions are both healthy and informative. Recognize that some group exercises might be inappropriate for people of certain religions or beliefs.

Another important task of the group leader is to listen attentively for clues on how to help group members recognize new possibilities for coping within their belief systems (Prest & Keller, 1993). By understanding how the client's life is influenced by his or her belief system, the leader can comprehend whether the system supports or offers alternatives to presenting problems (Joyce & Taylor, 1990).

If the leader feels that the elder is using spiritual beliefs to sustain negative thinking or isolating behaviors, then another approach outside group is preferred. Avoid challenging the validity of an elder's spirituality either within group or in an individual session. Make every effort to bring in a pastor, rabbi, priest, shaman, medicine man, or minister who represents the elder's belief system. Working as a team, the elder, the group leader, and the spiritual advisor hear the concerns of both client and leader. After making the connection and demonstrating positive regard, the leader disengages from the session and leaves the elder and the spiritual advisor to deal with the spiritual issues. In this way, the leader acknowledges the importance of the elder's beliefs without attempting to confuse roles by playing the part of both therapist and spiritual advisor. This is a sound approach even if the therapist is trained in theology or shares the same spiritual beliefs as the elder. Dual relationships exist in many places that are not apparent at first glance. Beware, this is one of them!

RITUALS

Incorporating rituals within the GSE groups is another important element in reflection and adaptation to the later stages of life. Reminiscing or reenacting significant rituals serves as a link between the concrete and the symbolic (Cole, 1990). Familiar social and religious rituals honor, affirm, or validate an experience. Even everyday personal rituals such as a preferred order of putting on clothing organizes tasks in a way that is individually satisfying. If such a simple ritual or system reduces anxiety and increases likelihood of task completion, then those complex or symbolic rituals can reduce existential anxiety.

SPIRITUALITY: RITUALS OF PASSAGE

Goals: Marking changes of time in a positive way improves self-esteem.

Process: On the marker board or overhead are a list of familiar rituals such as confirmation, quinceaños, bar or bat mitzvah, marriage, graduation, and retirement party. If possible, show pictures of the rituals important to various cultural groups. The leader initiates exploration of what is similar and different about each ritual the group wants to discuss. If not already mentioned, the leader comments on rituals as being symbolic of change. In life changes, rituals of passage mark an achievement that earns elevation to a new status. On the marker board, the leader draws a timeline from birth to death with lines at regular intervals marking decades. The group suggests other rituals and the approximate time these occur. After completing the timeline, group members consider what their last ritual of passage was and what ritual remains. Higher functioning groups are usually quick to see that the only remaining ritual of passage is a funeral, one in which they have no active part. The leader redirects attention to the timeline and asks members to talk about which rituals of passage were the most significant turning points in their lives. Was there anything about the ritual that was special? Were the sights, sounds, dress, setting, or other sensory elements important to the ritual? If they could relive one important ritual of passage, which would it be?

Outcomes: Rituals of passage are important in every culture as outward symbols of life change. Reflecting on those times and the resulting changes can be very satisfying because the individual involved is usually showered with attention and good will. This modality recalls, recreates, or creates ceremonies that provide social and familial connections, merging of self with beliefs, and formalizing connections with others.

Equipment list: Marker board. Photos of rituals of passage.

SPIRITUALITY: RITUALS OF WELCOME

Goals: Elders create rituals of welcome into senior years.

Process: This is an excellent follow-up to discussion on rituals of passage that is most effectively accomplished by a higher functioning, cohesive group. The leader asks the group to recall what event or occurrence marked their entry into senior adulthood and when it happened. Was this passage marked by getting a Social Security check, registering for Medicare, retiring from work, or being eligible for senior discount cards at the pharmacy? The leader invites the group to create a ritual of welcome into senior adulthood or to congregate living (if held in a facility). This project usually takes several sessions to plan, prepare, and perform. Group members are asked what talents each might contribute to the ritual, such as singing, speaking, greeting, or arranging the program. As much as possible, the leader needs to step aside and empower the group to take control of the ritual. The leader continually poses questions, takes notes, keeps a reminder list, and coordinates resources. For example, if the group wants a formal candlelight ceremony, the leader calls a local church to borrow choir robes and candle stands. If the group decides to invite family or friends, the leader negotiates with the facility for space and time as well as volunteers to address invitations. With the group's permission, the leader takes photos or a videotape as a lasting memory that can be shared at a future session. The ritual of welcome may range from a half hour to an hour. Most facilities will allow (and even sponsor) a reception afterwards. The group may agree to have the leader transcribe or script their ritual of welcome, which can become a facility tradition in welcoming newcomers quarterly or semiannually.

Outcomes: Welcome rituals for elders in their community or nursing home allow them to do what is not currently done, that is, reframe the lifestyle changes from being an albatross to an adventure with a positive beginning. The more the group takes ownership of the ritual of welcome, the more they benefit from the result. Too often elders are taken to events and not given the opportunity to be involved in the event's creation. Given artistic freedom, the rituals will take on the personality of the group: sometimes festive and sometimes serious, but always meaningful to its creative force.

Equipment list: Marker board. Other items as requested by the group.

SPIRITUALITY: LIFE-CHANGING MOMENTS

Goals: Reflecting on events that radically changed an individual's life is a way to review the roads not taken.

Process: The leader may begin by reading Robert Frost's poem "The Road not Taken." In this poem, a critical decision was reached and a life-changing choice was made. Inform group members that you will read the poem slowly a second time. While you are reading, each member is to try to recall an important choice that resulted in a major life change. Draw a line symbolizing a road with a fork to indicate two paths. As each member shares a personal story, create visual impact by writing a brief description of each of the paths. Seeing the words connected with the choices is a strong image. Allow members to discuss both positive and negative choices. Direct the attention of lower functioning groups toward recalling decisions that involved positive choices and satisfactory results.

Outcomes: Choices made and chances missed are increasingly important to elders who feel that they have no opportunity to compensate for mistakes. Listen to these concerns and give a forum for questioning false. beliefs or affirming the difficult choices

Equipment list: Robert Frost's poem "The Road not Taken." Marker board.

SPIRITUALITY: POSTCARDS FROM ETERNITY

Goals: Group members contemplate existence beyond this life.

Process: The leader brings in several vacation postcards with the typical "having a great time, wish you were here" message written on them. Then each member is given blank postcards on which to write a note from the future to a special person. The future place is whatever or wherever each individual believes that his or her spirit will reside after death. Everyone is free to express personal religious or philosophical views. The message needs to be short and directed to the person to whom it is addressed. If the group is hesitant to begin writing, take time to discuss various members' ideas and concerns.

Outcomes: Persons who are satisfied with their views of existence after death generally write positive comments and encouragement or advice for loved ones on how to join them. Discomfort with death and lack of spiritual resolution is evident from postcards with negative, angry messages or a refusal to participate. Extreme reactions indicate the need for individual counseling on resolving life issues or pastoral counseling by the person's spiritual advisor.

Equipment list: Oversized postcards and markers.

SPIRITUALITY: SPIRITUAL COMPANIONS

Goals: The focus is on spiritual companions as symbolic of protection for humans.

Process: Various cultures have an image of spiritual companions that appear in stories and religious folklore such as angels, ancestors, mythological characters, or saints. The leader introduces the topic by asking each member to share his or her perception of spiritual companions and whether this is an important element of their spiritual belief system. Display some pictures, dolls, or other representations of positive spiritual companions. Are spiritual companions former humans or different types of beings? What is the function of a spiritual companion? Are there special people from your past or present who seemed to show up at just the right moment to offer help? Can you be a comfort or encouragement to someone?

Outcomes: Beliefs about positive spiritual forces are another means of coping with infirmity and loneliness. Sharing those beliefs are meant to verbalize and affirm an individual's beliefs and discover that they may be shared by others.

Equipment list: Pictures, statuettes, tree decorations, dolls, or other representations of spiritual companions such as angels, mythological characters, saints, or ancestors.

SPIRITUALITY: UNSEEN COMFORTS

Goals: Using visualization, group members identify the unseen comforts that help them cope with difficulty.

Process: For this activity, the leader must be appropriately qualified and trained in visualization. The group is given a preview of what will take place during this personal journey. With whatever approach the leader is skilled in, begin the relaxation and exploration. The intent is for members to identify several difficult times in their lives, yet keep the focus on who or what was the unseen comfort that helped them in a time of problems. Keep attention on the comforting presence. Is the unseen comforter the same in several situations or different? Does the comforter have a name? Is it a living person or a spiritual being? Is that unseen comfort available in the present? What are some ways to experience the unseen comfort at a time of need? Teach a basic relaxation strategy before the close of the session.

Outcomes: Visualization is a way to unlock coping skills that seem beyond present abilities. Each person's experience is unique and need not be shared with the group. At the close of each session, members are requested to share how they presently feel on the basis of what they experienced or learned during the exercise.

Equipment list: Instrumental tape with pacing suitable for visualization. Cassette player.

SPIRITUALITY: SPIRITUAL LEGACY

Goals: Group members consider how continuity across generations in their lives is related to transmission of values and spirituality.

Process: The leader introduces the concept of legacy or reads a brief work on legacy. Using a four-generation genogram form (in the form of a large poster or drawn on a marker board), the leader explains the form as group members follow along on preprinted pages. The four generations are labeled as grandparents, parents, identified person with his or her generation, and children. This spiritual genogram is not as detailed as typical genograms. Giving dates, ages, and every name are not important. The spiritual genogram is completed by writing the names of family members from each generation who were most influential in teaching, changing, or establishing spiritual or religious beliefs for the identified person. To get the most from this project, the leader may direct the group in working on one generation per session. Ask group members to talk about the person within a given generation whom they thought was spiritual and why. How did that person share spirituality with others? Were there any conflicts evident between spoken beliefs and actions? Did they accept or reject that person's spiritual views? What spiritual concepts did they transmit to their children? Do their children practice what they taught or something different? How do they feel about that? Beside each significant name on the spiritual genogram, write a comment or a plus or a minus sign to indicate a positive or negative contribution to developing present understanding of spirituality. Draw genogram lines to indicate broken, strained, or close relationships with spiritual mentors and the identified person.

Outcomes: Higher functioning groups can resolve many unspoken issues from their lives with this critical look at spiritual values. As typical with genograms, family patterns and relationships become evident in ways formerly not acknowledged.

Equipment list: Spiritual genogram pages, marker board and boldly colored markers, or overhead projector.

SPIRITUALITY: SPIRITUAL SYMBOLS

Goals: Exploration of the outward signs that describe or represent spirituality.

Process: The leader poses the question of how spirituality is shown in nonverbal ways with symbols. Show photos of spiritual symbols from various faiths such as crosses, fish, prayer beads, Star of David, and candles. After viewing the photos, the group responds by sharing what beliefs they associate with each symbol. The leader can note responses on the marker board. Is a symbol enough to fully identify a belief? Can symbols stand for more than one belief? The symbolism of candles and light has many meanings; what does it mean to each group member? What are some other symbols or nonverbal signs that are part of spiritual beliefs? Why are visual symbols used to signify an unseen concept like spirituality?

Outcomes: Elders generally cling to tradition and the outward signs of those beliefs. This discussion gives thought to how a person uses spiritual symbols and what that may communicate to others. What may also be found here is how much external symbols relate to external locus of control compared with persons of intense internal spirituality who rely less on symbols to express spirituality.

Equipment list: Marker board and boldly colored markers. Photos of various types of religious symbols or artifacts.

SPIRITUALITY: MORTALITY AND REALITY

Goals: Dealing with the death of a new or less involved group member.

Process: Before group, the leader obtains as much information as possible (within confidentiality limits) about the group member's death. The questions most often asked by groups are these: Did she or he die peacefully? In his or her own room or at the hospital? Were any family members or friends in attendance? What are the arrangements for a funeral or memorial? At the beginning of the group, the leader announces a change in plans for today in order to honor the deceased group member. After giving basic information about the circumstances of the death and any known memorial arrangements, the leader invites questions. Without taking too much time with details or allowing a round of deathbed stories to surface, the leader asks the group to join in saying something about the deceased person that was not said before. Comments often take this form: "I didn't know him well and I wish I had had more time to talk to him" or "Even though he was new to our group, he had such a happy laugh that it made me laugh just to hear him." Each person may speak or choose to pass. The leader closes with a final positive comment about the deceased person. To bring the focus from mortality back to reality, the leader encourages each person to turn to the person on his or her right (and so on around the group) and say something positive or complimentary. The group may choose to end by singing, particularly a song that was known to be liked by the deceased member.

Outcomes: The death of any group member must be acknowledged in a respectful way. When the deceased was not well-known or popular, others may feel guilty about their lack of connection to this person. Sharing positive comments about the deceased and about each other affirms them all.

Equipment list: None.

SPIRITUALITY: IT'S HARD TO SAY GOODBYE

Goals: Finding a way to cope with the death of a popular, active group member.

Process: As explained in the "Mortality and Reality" exercise, the leader brings information to the group in announcing the death. Bring plenty of tissues because when the deceased person was highly regarded by the group, tears may flow freely. The leader suggests that today's group be a special kind of memorial. An empty chair, representing the missing member, is placed in the center of the group. Each member takes a turn saying the farewell that they never had the opportunity to say. Some touching farewells from GSE groups have included "Dance till dawn everyday until I get there to join you" and "Good wind with smooth sailing" followed by a military salute from a fellow veteran. As a symbol of the enduring memory of the deceased, the leader brings the empty chair back into the circle, explaining that the friendship and joy of knowing this person remains with the group always. Then, following the leader's example, each person recalls a brief story or tells what they considered special about the deceased.

Outcomes: Acknowledging the loss of a member who was special to the group needs to be done in a way that allows adequate expression of tribute in a personal way by all members. At the passing of a man whose wife was a frequent, cheerful visitor to the facility, group members asked the GSE leader to transcribe their farewell messages and present them to the widow as a token of their sympathy. Another memorable farewell was for a 90-year-old woman who had had a quick wit. Group members felt it only fitting to share a final laugh with her by recalling her favorite jokes as part of their memorial to her.

Equipment list: None.

Chapter 11

Art and Expression

Art belongs with life itself.

—Max Eastman

Art and expression are inseparable twins of human emotions that appeal to all ages. Every culture and society produces art that reflects its lifestyle, values, and experiences. Elders in group programs have seen a number of different artistic styles representative of social, cultural, and political changes during their 60-plus years of life. During their lifetimes, art became both varied and plentiful. In the United States, art is so easily accessible that it practically fades into the surroundings. How often is critical notice given by passersby to the poster reprints at the discount stores, the original unheralded landscapes at craft fairs, or the painted-on-velvet portrait of a dog or deceased rock star hawked from the street corner? Although not exactly in the same category as the original masterpieces displayed at the local museum or university exposition, there is art and expression represented in all these examples. Though there are distinct differences in quality, the joy of expression and sharing of self is valid in all forms of art.

The Greek philosopher Aristotle believed that art represents not the "outward appearance of things, but their inward significance." This is an excellent summation of GSE's goals for art and expression within the geriatric group. The art that is produced or examined is for therapeutic, not critical, purposes. Even when the art is created by group members, the intrinsic value is in what is felt (inward significance) than what is seen by others (outward appearance).

G. L. Lewis (1979) presented an intriguing connection between the Adlerian concept of humans as striving toward social regard, love, and work as essential to understanding the needs of institutionalized elders. The desire to work and be productive is both instinctive and socially promoted by their generation (the work ethic). Therapeutic art activities can replace work as a new means of being productive. Considering that the word *art* is derived from the Latin *ars*, meaning "skill," this connection between art and work touches a key conflict of aging represented in the loss of work as a means of self-expression and validation.

ART FOR ELDER GROUPS

The socializing aspect of art in geriatric group work is as significant as its projective potential (Docherty, 1986). In children's art groups, cooperating to produce an art project tends to reduce feelings of isolation and foster a sense of belonging (Swenson, 1991). GSE groups have found the same results of cooperation with art in elder art groups.

The approaches to art therapy are both active (creating art) and passive (responding to art). Depending on the group's dexterity and interest, this may include (a) viewing and discussing classic art reprints; (b) drawing, painting, or clay sculpting; and (c) making collages on a theme or as an expression of feelings. The types of activities can be varied or repeated for maximum effect. Each approach offers commonalities of socialization, response, and reaction as well as differences in application, involvement, and emotional content. The introduction of painting in elder groups encourages use of creative problem-solving skills related to decisions about the art project that may hone those skills for use in other situations (Harrison, 1980). Again the product is both visual (outward appearance) and internal (inward significance of enhanced problem-solving skills). Less hands-on applications of the visual arts in group are nonetheless expressive because the works of others are presented. Art therapy is also effective for elders who have difficulty verbalizing and those with speech impairments (Weiss, 1984). With developmentally disabled older adults, Harlan (1990) found art therapy to be a suitable replacement for meaningful activities or work and a means of improving self-esteem and autonomous functioning.

As with bibliotherapy, art can be a means of seeing beyond the self or seeing the self from a distance. For even cognitively impaired members, art evokes memories or feelings of tranquility and familiarity. These group members are easily frustrated with cognitively based activities and are often more attentive to the pleasures of the sensory and affective aspects of visual arts (Johnson, Lahey, & Shore, 1992). Art can penetrate the cognitive confusion of Alzheimer's disease and comparable conditions to provide a structure for expressing emotions and counteracting social isolation in ways that are stimulating without overloading capacity (Harlan, 1993; Wald, 1986).

THE LEADER'S ROLE

In art and expression groups, great technique is not a factor for either the leader or the group. Leaders do not have to be great artists to apply this modality. Whenever possible, consultation or coleadership with a trained art therapist is highly beneficial. The leader may also find technical assistance from a community volunteer or a college art student who can help organize the supplies, demonstrate projects, and guide group members in completing their artwork. Never be hesitant to learn a new art technique along with the group. Allow the group to encourage each other and the leader while facing the common problem of struggling with running watercolors and misplaced paint spots.

Always be aware of group members' skills, dexterity, vision, and cognitive level in order to match their capabilities to the project and the tools. For example, GSE art groups enjoyed finger painting but disdained painting with brushes. A revelation while at the hardware store selecting brushes to paint wood trim resulted in a group leader buying a handful of 1-inch and 2-inch brushes for the group. The next brush painting session was enjoyed by all. What was the magic? The larger interior house-painting brushes were easier to hold and control, thus making the project less irritating than with the typical, smaller fine art brushes. If preparation time and cleanup are factors, consider using large washable markers instead of paint and brushes.

Another useful in vivo experience was in learning to offer a smaller number of very distinct colors for each project. Although Tate and Allen's study (1985) found that elder men and women significantly preferred light colors to dark colors, GSE groups responded best to primary colors and bold derivatives. Pastels and pale colors are difficult for some elders to distinguish.

Preparation is another important aspect. Inform the group or the nursing staff in advance of painting, sculpting, or drawing sessions, which can be messy. Spills and drops happen even for experienced artists. Plastic or fabric art aprons for each member avoids the crisis of ruining a favorite garment. Also take precautions to protect the floor, and cover art tables with old newspaper or inexpensive plastic drop cloths.

In responding to the group projects, the rule is that the effort is even more valuable than the result. Elder art done with shaking hands or reduced vision can be as much a reflection of feelings or words that cannot be expressed as is the work of master artists. In sharing their work, the group's emotions may run extremely high and inner conflicts may surface, or it can be a playful, relaxing time. Leaders need to be prepared for both possibilities.

ART AND EXPRESSION:
EMOTIONS REFLECTED IN ART

Goals: Finding emotion in art requires bringing to the surface one's own feelings.

Process: The leader shows photos or slides of great paintings in which there is strong emotional content. Avoid showing art in which the strong emotional content is violent or fearful. Take time to allow each group member to view the visual image and think about it. Ask for comments on what the message communicates to each person. What emotions are visible? Do the emotions seem to fit the overall situation shown in the image? What emotions are felt by the viewer?

Outcomes: Feeling the strong feelings captured by the artist can be safer than expressing one's own feelings.

Equipment list: Color photos or slide projector with slides. Note: Local museums, colleges, and libraries may loan a collection for viewing.

ART AND EXPRESSION: PAINTING

Goals: A way to appreciate painting is to try it firsthand.

Process: The leader or an artistically talented volunteer explains each step of the project. The idea is not to make a great painting, but to feel what an artist feels when combining colors on a blank canvas. An assistant or another group member can help guide the hands of a person with limited dexterity or a visual impairment. The visually impaired person may prefer to finger paint, enjoying the feel of applying the paint on canvas. (Note: Be certain to use paints that are safe and suitable for finger painting.) Talk about the sensory aspects of mixing the colors, touching the paints, and spreading paint on the surface. Make swirls, dabs, dots, and lines with paint. Anyone can create a simple design such as a rainbow and clouds. Emphasize that the opportunity to feel how a painting is done is more important than the completed picture.

Outcomes: The outcome here is not the finished picture, but the actual experience of painting. Group members often surprise themselves in finding this enjoyable.

Equipment list: Poster paints, watercolors, or fingerpaints. Small canvas or art paper. Brushes with wide or easy-grip handles and cleanup supplies.

ART AND EXPRESSION: PAINT THE MUSIC

Goals: Painting is the means for expressing feelings about music.

Process: The leader brings instrumental music tapes with different tempos and styles (i.e., classical, swing, slow jazz, and waltz). The group is instructed to listen to the music and paint any form, color, or design that gives a visual image to the sounds. There is no pressure to create a picture. The intent is for each person to relate colors with sounds and forms with musical style. The music is changed at regular intervals, 5–10 minutes per interval. Individuals can choose to paint on one poster board or use separate boards for each musical tempo. As the music plays, the leader periodically and softly reminds the group of the objective to hear and feel the music, then find the colors and forms to express those feelings. In a follow-up session, invite members to show their paintings. Talk about what kind of images each person gets from different types of music. Do sharp lines, zigzag lines, smooth curves, or angles relate to a certain musical style? How can bright as opposed to dark colors be used to match musical passages? Did painting the music give way to any new feelings about the music?

Outcomes: Painting and music are additional ways to stimulate expression of feelings. Higher functioning groups are more successful at completing this project and understanding the connection between feelings and form. However, low-functioning groups enjoy painting to music with less direction and more free form.

Equipment list: Poster paint, watercolors, or finger paints. Either 11-inch × 17-inch or quarter-size poster board or art paper. Brushes with wide or easy-grip handles and cleanup supplies. Cassettes with background music and cassette player.

ART AND EXPRESSION: SOFT SCULPTURE

Goals: A way to understand sculpture is to experience it firsthand.

Process: The leader displays photos or examples of sculptures to the group. To experience the sculptor's feelings at making something from a shapeless mass, each member is given a container of soft dough. Initially, direct each person to squeeze, pat, or roll the dough with his or her eyes closed, thinking only of the sensory perceptions. Using the dough, the leader shows how to roll three sections into balls and stack to resemble a snowman. The leader asks everyone to make a sculpture of anything. Cookie cutters are passed around the table for use in the project or for those who seem intimidated by unstructured creativity. Before finishing, affix each project to a block base and label with the artist's name. With the artist's permission, keep the projects in the group room to enjoy or display them in the community room.

Outcomes: Adults have just as much fun with soft dough projects as children. The result is not as important as the variety of sensory, visual, and creative stimuli that accompany this project.

Equipment list: Children's soft dough modeling material in various colors. Cookie cutters in many shapes. A small wooden block as base for each soft sculpture. Pictures or examples of sculpture.

ART AND EXPRESSION: SCENE DRAWN BY GROUP

Goals: The group cooperates to produce a creative project.

Process: As a visual demonstration of cooperation and creativity, the group produces a large scene, with each person making a contribution. Before beginning, the leader explains the basic steps of deciding what type of scene and elements of the scene. Members work individually or as teams on different areas of the scene. Any members with artistic talent and interest are encouraged to help direct the project. For example, the group decides to create a country scene. A light pencil line is drawn to distinguish middle ground and background. The group discusses what elements best display the country feeling: winding road, bridge, barn, farmhouses, orchard, crops in a field, windmill, and so forth. Each member is assigned a part in the picture. Even physically challenged members can participate, with assistance in guiding their hands to create sweeping clouds or dab red dots for apples on the trees. To avoid tiring the group, work with the paper or poster board on tables. After the work is complete, tape it to the wall for all to appreciate. This project may take several group sessions or with a simple scene may be done in teams in one session.

Outcomes: This project gets everyone involved in decision making, creating, and performing the role of an artist. Working together builds group cohesiveness.

Equipment list: Wide roll of white wrapping paper or poster board panels. Crayons or washable markers.

ART AND EXPRESSION: SEASONAL COLLAGE

Goals: The group creates a seasonal collage, combining various materials to express a common theme.

Process: The leader talks briefly about the season that is the subject of this group. Reading a poem or listening to related music further establishes images of the season. Group members gather around tables, working in pairs or groups of four. Each minigroup discusses how to express the seasonal theme in a positive way. For example, spring may be portrayed by one group as "a time of renewal" and by another group as "flower fantasy." Each minigroup is directed to use any or all of the items available to communicate their chosen theme with colors and materials in a collage. While working, the leader engages members in discussing how they plan to use certain materials, texture combinations, or colors to convey a feeling. Lower functioning groups often work better separately with clear, simple instructions from the leader and a given theme. With all groups, the leader can use volunteers to assist in cutting, gluing, or operating the hot glue gun as members work. This speeds up the project and is safer. This project can be done over several sessions. Plan a final or follow-up session as a presentation time for the group to view and comment on what they feel or see in each other's work.

Outcomes: Translating feelings into a collage does not require artistic skill or a high degree of digital dexterity. This three-dimensional, multitextured collage is a satisfying sensory experience with a creative result.

Equipment list: Wide roll of white wrapping paper or poster board. Crayons or washable markers, scissors, and glue. Old magazines for cutouts or precut pictures, fabric pieces, ribbon, beads, leaves, and twigs. Sponges with poster paints are used for overlay and accents.

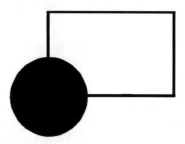

ART AND EXPRESSION: CIRCLES AND FORMS

Goals: Members use shapes to express feelings of inclusion or exclusion.

Process: On a large marker board, the leader draws examples of how shapes and colors can represent concepts. For example, circles intertwined show a bond as with beads in a chain or symbolize people linking arms and walking together. Give pencils, paper, and templates to each member. Let them practice outlining the templates with pencils. Then give each a sheet of clean paper and direct each person to select a form (circle, square, triangle) that represents themselves. They draw that form in the top area of the blank page and color it with a color that expresses how they feel today, then select one or two forms (same or different) that represent other group members. Those forms are drawn near or just below the form for self and colors for these forms assigned. On the lower part of the page or on a clean page, each person uses the forms to show the self in relation to this group. The actual number of forms and group members is not important. What is significant is looking at the individual's feelings about inclusion in or exclusion from this group. After everyone is finished, talk generally about how it feels to be part of a group. What makes them feel accepted? How do other people communicate acceptance to them in nonverbal ways? Drawing self and the group can be done by a person at any functioning level. Using the drawings as a springboard to discussion of intergroup relationships is suitable only for higher functioning members in groups who have some cohesiveness or have spent a longer time together.

Outcomes: The leader learns much about each member's sense of belonging from the design and colors used in these drawings. Members whose work shows separation from others, dismal colors or forms, and overall feelings of discomfort need individual attention from the leader before continuing in group.

Equipment list: Templates in several forms and sizes. Colored pencils or large writing pencils. Marker board.

ART AND EXPRESSION: SPONGE PAINTING

Goals: Simple sponge painting requires minimal skill and produces interesting expressions of color and form.

Process: Workstations with supplies are prepared for each group member around a table. The leader demonstrates how to use the sponges for painting by dropping them into the paint and then onto the paper. Group members are directed to use the sponge shapes and letters to cover the blank surface with an original design that is personally appealing.

Outcomes: This project is simple to do with or without artistic ability. The color blending and shapes may be very well defined or random, according to individual style. Completing the project is entertaining and offers some sensory stimulation.

Equipment list: Precut sponges in various shapes and letters. Half-size poster board or quarter yard of strong, tight-weave cloth. Disposable pie tins or recycled margarine containers. Washable paints. Cleanup supplies.

ART AND EXPRESSION: PAIN MANAGEMENT

Goals: Using drawing to express and manage physical pain.

Process: Many elders suffer from some level of physical decline or pain. With reduced activity, an excessive amount of attention is given to discomfort rather than to establishing a sense of mastery. The leader initiates this project by discussing how difficult it is to explain pain. Using the marker board and colored markers, the leader illustrates a common pain description such as "a red-hot sun, with sharp rays extending all around." Engage the group in a discussion of what moderates the sun's heat. One option is to draw blue clouds around the sun and cover the rays with raindrops. This is a cooling image that makes the heat more manageable. Instruct each person to draw a shape, form, or color that represents pain on the paper. As each person presents his or her pain drawing, the group brainstorms ideas for another image to moderate the pain. After everyone draws a cooling or soothing image over the pain picture, discuss how this visualization can be used to master pain.

Outcomes: This visualization exercise supported by art reinforces a sense of control that is often a critical issue for elders.

Equipment list: Art paper, drawing pencils and crayons, or washable markers. Marker board.

ART AND EXPRESSION: MESSAGE IN THE MASTERS

Goals: Group members explore nonverbal messages communicated through great works of art.

Process: The leader introduces this activity as a group effort to identify the obvious and hidden meanings in well-known artwork. This activity is more effective after the group has done some painting or other creative project. View a picture, consider the name of the work, and what is apparent at first glance. For example, Leonardo da Vinci's Mona Lisa is a familiar image. The painting of the woman and her famous smile are well-known, but does she actually seem happy? If not happiness, what other emotion might be behind her smile? What does the landscape scene in the background tell about this woman or her life? Are there any other elements in the picture that communicate a message? These are examples of questions that stimulate discussion on what group members see and feel about each picture. The leader may write summary comments on the marker board or keep the discussion free flowing. Continue with this format to discuss several art prints from different historical periods and styles.

Outcomes: For some members, classic art is pleasurable and stimulates memories of times and places from their past. Visual acuity is a greater hurdle than cognitive functioning in participating in this activity. Shorter attention spans of lower functioning groups suggest that discussion remain on a general level—the obvious subjects in the picture and feelings derived from viewing it.

Equipment list: Library book, prints, or slides of well-known art by da Vinci, Renoir, Monet, and other master artists.

Chapter 12

Remotivation

Skill to do comes of doing.

—Ralph Waldo Emerson

Remotivation groups seek to restore an incentive for greater participation in the activities of daily living and, if possible, creative pursuits beyond mere existence. This technique was developed for psychiatric patients from the ideas of Dorothy Smith, who worked as a volunteer at Pennsylvania State Hospital in the mid-1950s. The concept attracted the attention of the American Psychiatric Association, which, along with Smith, Kline & French Laboratories, promulgated remotivation groups in hospitals and long-term care facilities around the country (Robinson, no date).

Toepfer, Bicknell, and Shaw (1974) suggested that remotivation is closely akin to behavioral therapies in that both aim for certain operationally desired behaviors and work toward meeting the goals defined for each patient. Over years of clinical application, remotivation has grown beyond a behavioral foundation to include affective elements. Observing elders' progress in remotivation is like peeling an onion. The outer layers are tough and seem unconnected to the core. Further into the layers is a concrete level of thinking that distances self and others from emotionality. Near the core are feelings, memories, and values that are suppressed until the individual discovers reasons to be involved in the present and care about the future. Part of shedding the layers of ambivalence involves reminiscence, sensory awareness, and socialization within the group.

From a functional perspective, remotivation is sometimes linked with reality orientation. Clearly, there are differences in purpose and theory. Reality orientation is used with confused elders and psychiatric patients who are disoriented as to person, place, and time. Reality orientation is definitely different than reality therapy. The latter was developed by Glasser (1965) to foster social responsibility and self-reliance in delinquent adolescents. Folsom (1968) is credited with developing reality orientation for rehabilitation of geropsychiatric hospital patients. Key components were based on consistent repetition by all staff members of the patient's name; the day, time, and place; and directions around the unit and on calmly yet firmly stating requests.

GSE'S ECLECTIC APPROACH

GSE's approach to remotivation incorporates some of the elements of reality orientation into remotivation groups. This eclectic mixture of remotivation and reality orientation spiced with reminiscence and sensory awareness is also used with varying degrees of effectiveness in other group programs (Bledsoe & Lutz-Ponder, 1986; Forsythe, 1989; Hern & Weis, 1991; Maloney & Daily, 1986; Zimpfer, 1987).

Every GSE remotivation session begins with a simplified reality orientation wherein the leader greets every member by name, states the day of the week and date, shows a color weather map from the newspaper (cold shown in blue, hot progressively in shades of yellow to orange) and asks questions about the weather. Before beginning any activity, the leader explains briefly what activity is planned and precisely what members need to do to participate. As a group becomes more cohesive, the leader may declare an open period of 5 or 10 minutes for anyone to make a positive statement to the group or to raise any issues for discussion. Allowing open time is counterproductive with cognitively impaired, confused, or wandering persons. Lower functioning groups need structure and respond to repeated reality orientation during the activity.

Whether beginning with subtle reality orientation or reframing negative images of self and circumstance, GSE groups progress through a series of stated topics to elicit individual responses and eventually to group interaction. As with traditional remotivation therapy, topics and activities are alternated. Discussions and participatory exercises are geared toward a specific theme. Themes may be as basic as performing an activity of daily living or more thought provoking as family holiday traditions and travel experiences.

GROUP RESPONSES

Adaptation to present circumstances and resulting change in attitudes about self and others that lead to acceptance are major goals. Secondary goals are defined by the needs of each individual in group. A rambling talker who monopolizes conversation without saying anything meaningful may find his or her energies redirected toward hands-on activities to focus energies on a task. The shy, suspicious newcomer who prefers to ignore others in favor of solitary activities is given a working partner or some type of encouragement to verbally interact with others. The leader gleans ideas for goals from the facility treatment team report, from family or physician recommendations, and by monitoring individuals within group.

Remotivation applied in the group format is useful as a means of increasing opportunities for socialization. GSE has also used a variation on remotivation as an adjustment group for newcomers to a long-term care facility. Remotivation groups provide an entry-level trial for determining the suitability of newcomers for other more active or affective groups.

Resistance and apathy are equally difficult to manage as members deal with present circumstances. Traditional remotivation groups meet for a stated period, such as 12 or 14 weeks, leading toward closure. GSE groups and other nursing home groups work with the same patients for a longer period of time or at additional times owing to losses in functioning, coping, or adaptation to new circumstances. Thus, GSE remotivation groups are more open ended, allowing members to flow in and out according to their progress and needs.

LEADER'S ROLE IN REMOTIVATION

The most effective remotivation leaders are directive, encouraging, and capable of conducting task-oriented groups. These highly structured activities also require more outside group effort in planning, organizing, and preparing materials. While conducting groups, the leader continually monitors and guides each member toward achievement of individual goals. Thus, remotivation groups place a large demand on the leader's skills and energies. A larger group (more than eight people) functions better with coleaders who share duties. Coleaders alternate presenting the activity and monitoring members' progress, or coleaders share presentation responsibilities yet divide the members for monitoring and redirection.

In addition to stated individual goals, remotivation leaders look for overall positive responses from group members, which include but are not limited to the following: (a) active listening, (b) verbalizing appropriately in discussions, (c) attentiveness to the activity, (d) ability to remain on task, (e) responding to reality cues, (f) accepting redirection, (g) making an effort to communicate with other group members, and (h) demonstrating or expressing positive feelings in group.

Effectiveness of remotivation and reality orientation are widely debated in the literature without consensus. GSE leaders working in long-term-care geriatric facilities agree with the findings of Murphy, Conley, and Hernandez (1994) that remotivation activities are simple to implement, promote interaction among members, and are rewarding experiences for the leaders. Overall, GSE remotivation groups with high- and low-functioning members have been a nurturing ground for positive change and renewal of social skills in the small-group environment.

REMOTIVATION: MEET AND GREET

Goals: Giving attention to each individual and his or her interests helps the group begin to know one another.

Process: The leader welcomes each person on his or her arrival and assists in finding a seat or wheelchair space in the circle. When everyone is seated in the circle, the leader puts on a name tag and introduces him- or herself, then brings a name tag to each person, repeats his or her name, and asks the group to greet the person by name. Next, the leader tells a basic preference about him- or herself, such as "My favorite color is blue," and writes *blue* on the second line of the name tag. The leader goes around the group, repeating each person's name and asking about his or her favorite color. The member can write that information on the name tag, or the leader can offer to do so. Next, the leader repeats this process with a third piece of identifying information, such as "My home state is Tennessee." As a way of incorporating the information and recognizing each person, the leader then turns to the person on his or her left and says "I want to introduce Mary. Her favorite color is yellow and she is from Georgia." Next it's Mary's turn to introduce the person to her left, and so on around the group, back to the leader. When this exercise is repeated with the same participants, solicit different information to complete the second and third lines.

Outcomes: Acknowledging members by name and giving attention to any aspect of their uniqueness is uplifting for self-esteem and may diminish fears of being lost within a group.

Equipment list: Large-print name tags with two additional lines. Washable markers.

REMOTIVATION: DAY AND MONTH

Goals: Orientation to time and place.

Process: The leader greets each person on arrival and gives name tag with first name printed in large letters. After all members are seated in a circle, the leader goes around the room, stating each name and inviting the group to greet each person by name. Directing attention to the large calendar, the leader circles this day with a brightly colored marker. Group members are asked to look at this mark and tell anything they can about this day and month. The leader confirms or corrects this by stating that, for example, "This is Monday, February 5" and pointing to the date, then asking if anyone has a birthday today or in this month. The birthdays are marked on the calendar (and the leader keeps notes of upcoming birthdays). Are there any other important events in the month of February? What and when? What do people associate with Monday (back to school, first day of work week, blue Monday, etc.)? During the discussion, the leader makes several casual repetitions of the day and month and points to the calendar for visual reference.

Outcomes: Becoming aware of day and date is important in restoring a sense of relationship to the rest of the world, from which institutionalized and mobility limited elders feel disconnected.

Equipment list: Marker board. Large calendar for current month. Brightly colored markers. Name tags.

REMOTIVATION: WEATHER AND SEASON

Goals: Orientation to time and place by associating weather with season.

Process: The leader welcomes each person on arrival and gives him or her a name tag with first name printed in large letters. If there is a window in the group room, the leader directs everyone's attention toward it. If not, the leader describes weather conditions outside and asks the group what season this appears to be. How do they know? What are the signs, colors, and feelings of the season? The most effective visual used in GSE groups is a color weather map from the local newspaper; *USA Today* has this type of map if the local paper does not. The national weather map uses colors to designate temperatures. Even low-functioning groups do well in relating blues with cool and reds with hot. The leader points on the map to the geographical location (city or state) of the group. What does the map say about this season? Can group members identify states where they previously lived and tell something about the weather there on the basis of the map colors? The leader then discusses any special events, holidays, or activities that are associated with this season.

Outcomes: Using the newspaper weather map as focus, members get a bigger picture of what is happening seasonally around the country rather than just what is outside their windows. Talking about seasonal weather in different areas brings out discussion of contrasts: snow may be falling in the Northeast while it is sunny in the southern coastal states. Weather, both extreme and normal, is a trigger for reminiscence. Members relate to where they have enjoyed spending time during the present season or other seasons (i.e., winter in Florida or Arizona, Maine for the summer, etc.). Weather may be associated with loneliness (snowbound winters), planting gardens (spring), going on vacation (summer), or returning to school (fall). Other reminiscences about surviving a hurricane, tornado, or ice storm can be turned from a negative to a positive by drawing out how the member overcame hardships and what was learned from the experience.

Equipment list: Color weather map from this day or previous day's newspaper. Name tags.

REMOTIVATION: CURRENT EVENTS

Goals: Enhance orientation toward present time by focusing on current events in the world outside one's immediate view.

Process: The leader greets each person on arrival and gives him or her a name tag. After everyone arrives, the leader writes on the board the day, date, and year. Group members are invited to comment on anything that is special about this date. The leader then shows the newspaper with the headlines of several articles highlighted with marker. Members can volunteer to read the headlines, or they may choose to pass. After reading the headline of each story, the leader inquires if anyone knows more about the story. The leader can summarize or read excerpts from a story, then invite comments. He or she can balance the serious news items with a few human interest stories, and avoid stories that hinge on violence and political or racial conflict. As each story is discussed, the leader asks group members if this story affects them and in what way. In repeating this group, the leader will discover that some groups are more interested in international news and others in local news. Think like a headline news service and try to cover a variety of different issues.

Outcomes: Few people of any age are without opinions about what is happening in their world. However, elders may appear as if they do not care about current events because their views are not sought. Keeping up with current issues encourages elders to think about problems and concerns outside themselves.

Equipment list: Local newspaper or current news magazine. Name tags. Marker board and markers.

REMOTIVATION: WHO'S NEWS?

Goals: Another way to enhance orientation toward present time through the people who are featured in the news.

Process: After greeting each member and giving him or her a name tag, the leader writes the day, date, and year on the board. Group members are informed that today attention will be focused on people who are making news. The leader clips newspaper or magazine photos of several well-known people (such as the president, leaders of other nations, sports figures, or actors), then shows a photo, identifies the person, and reads excerpts from the story. The group discusses how this person is making news or is caught up in a news event. Is this story consistent with prior knowledge of or beliefs about that news maker? If the news maker is not a public figure, as is common in a human interest story, what was learned about the person from reading the report?

Outcomes: Focusing on the famous public figures and unknown people in news events is another way to identify with what is happening in the world.

Equipment list: Newspaper or current news magazine. Marker board and markers.

REMOTIVATION: BEACH BALL TOSS

Goals: Group members relate through an activity.

Process: The leader greets each member and gives out name tags. After a brief time of mutual greetings, the leader explains a game that involves recognition of others. The leader gives each person a colored ribbon to wear loosely around the neck. Try to alternate the colors in a clockwise format so that red ribbons are at positions 12:00, 3:00, 6:00, and 9:00; blue ribbons at positions 1:00, 4:00, 7:00, and 10:00; and yellow ribbons at positions 2:00, 5:00, 8:00, and 11:00. Adjust for smaller numbers of participants. Play light instrumental music in the background. When the music begins, start passing one beach ball around the circle so everyone can handle it. This can be done standing or sitting; however, all participants need to be in the same position, either standing or sitting. The leader coordinates the ball toss by calling out the color. If the leader says "Pass to red," then the person with the ball can pass it to anyone who wears a red ribbon; if the leader says "Green pass to green," the ball is passed from one person with a green ribbon to someone else wearing the same color. A second beach ball can be added if manageable without frustration. Limit to one beach ball for lower functioning groups to reduce confusion and enhance concentration on the task. Divide the direction; first ask the member to point to another person wearing a red ribbon. After that is done, then ask that the ball be passed to the identified person with the red ribbon. Higher functioning groups or those with good arm mobility may enjoy a faster pace with two beach balls and more variety in calls. This game is active and keeps everyone involved. It's also a good break between more intense group activities or for a day when group members are fidgety or distracted.

Outcomes: Cooperating in a game that is easy for all to play is enjoyable and stimulates the cognitive–physical connections.

Equipment list: Several medium-sized, light beach balls in different primary colors. Instrumental music tape and cassette player. Colored ribbons. Name tags.

REMOTIVATION: LETTER-TO-WORD ASSOCIATION

Goals: Making connections between letters and words stimulates thinking and memory.

Process: After greeting each member and giving him or her a name tag, the leader introduces a new activity with the excitement of a television game show. One approach is to give an alphabet block to each person. Going around the room, the leader asks each member to show the block, say the letter, and then give one word that begins with the letter. The leader can repeat the word or write it on the marker board. Going around the room, each person gives a word beginning with that letter. The process is repeated for all members. A faster moving variation is for the leader to pick a letter, write it boldly on the board, then ask for word associations. Another option is for the leader to select a letter, get a response, then let the respondent select the next letter, and so on. Applauding efforts and creating excitement adds to the jovial atmosphere.

Outcomes: Sometimes the shy or reluctant members are more inclined to get involved in a game than in a discussion. It's easy for all levels. Even GSE's cognitively impaired groups participated enthusiastically in this activity with a slower pace and single-step directions.

Equipment List: Marker board. Optional: alphabet blocks with related pictures. Name tags.

REMOTIVATION: SHOW-AND-TELL

Goals: As members participate, they are encouraged to verbalize and also share the spotlight.

Process: The leader welcomes the group, distributes name tags, and introduces the activity. Each person is given a paper bag containing one commonly used item. The leader demonstrates the show-and-tell process in three steps: first, by looking into the bag and recognizing the item; second, by showing the item to the group and telling what it is; and third, by talking about some ways this item can be used. After the presenter is finished, she or he asks if anyone knows more ways to use the item. The process continues until all members have a turn at show-and-tell. If, on looking at the item, the member has any confusion or dislike, he or she can ask for another item. In discussing the items, there will be both factual content and reminiscence. The group applauds each person's effort.

Outcomes: This simple activity allows each person to be the expert and receive positive attention from the group.

Equipment list: A collection of lightweight, easy-to-hold common items such as a spiral notebook, teacup, kitchen timer, tape measure, trinket box, small flashlight, and garden tool. Paper bags. Name tags.

REMOTIVATION: TRANSPORTATION

Goals: Group members recall methods of transportation they have used and a related experience.

Process: After the welcome and mutual greetings, the leader displays a collection of photos or models that represent methods of transportation. If there are enough items, the leader gives one item or photo to each member. Taking turns, each member shows his or her item, names it, and talks about how it is used to transport people. After every member presents an item, the leader asks for names of unusual forms of transportation or those that have not been discussed and writes them on the board. These may include rapid transit subways, moving sidewalks in airports, elevators, escalators, ferry boats, and more exotic methods like the space shuttle, submarine, or hang glider. Discussion can evolve in several directions: reminiscence about favorite type of transportation in the past, a vehicle that was desired but never tried, or how popular means of transportation have changed during group members' lifetimes. The group may vote on their first, second, and third most popular transportation vehicles.

Outcomes: This topic is flexible and encompasses many common experiences. People of all levels of functioning seem to enjoy this discussion and tend toward reminiscences of first cars and interesting experiences in train or boat travel.

Equipment list: Pictures or models including cars, trains, trucks, buses, airplanes, helicopters, ships, and bicycles. Marker board and markers.

REMOTIVATION: ROCKS AND SHELLS

Goals: Group members identify and relate objects from nature to their sources.

Process: Following the welcome and greeting, the leader invites members to participate in this armchair nature exploration that will compare objects from the seashore with those from the mountains. The leader displays rocks and shells of different sizes, shapes, and varieties. Preparing large-type cards with a brief description of each item before group allows the group members to assist in presenting the items. As each type of rock or shell is passed around for inspection, the leader asks members to comment on how it looks, feels, and smells. Does it remind them of any personal experience? Have they ever collected rocks or shells? What are some ways to use rocks and shells for decorating or jewelry?

Outcomes: This activity brings familiar objects from nature that have sensory and reminiscence potential. People at all levels of functioning enjoy handling and discussing experiences with finding or collecting rocks and shells.

Equipment list: Labeled samples of rocks, granite, quartz, and shells. Library books with background information and photos of different types of rocks and shells.

Part Three

Financial Support
for Elder Groups

Chapter 13

Managed Payment Systems

Government, even in its best state, is but a necessary evil; in its worse state, an intolerable one.

—Thomas Paine, *Common Sense* (1776)

The passage of the law implementing Medicare (in 1965) opened the door for greater health care services to persons over 65. Five years later (in 1970), Chief Actuary Robert Myers sounded the warning that at present growth rates Medicare would be swallowed in a devastating deficit by 1995 (Feder, 1977). The Federal Hospital Insurance Trustees 1981 report was even more grim in the expectation of a severe deficit by 1991 (*Annual Report,* 1981). In spite of the doomsayers, the scope of Medicare coverage was significantly enlarged in 1972 with the addition of disabled persons and end-stage renal disease patients. As the 1990s arrived, so did the shadow of the grim reaper, with predictions of financial collapse looming ever closer to reality. Providers, beneficiaries, and politicians still search for that ultimate oxymoron, painless cost containment.

Various efforts to control rising Medicare costs have been tried since the early concerns over increased patient usage and decreasing resources arose. Both beneficiaries (patients) and providers (physicians and others) have been targets of political battles, cost containment, and benefits changes. Medicare's checkered past as relates to mental health providers is too lengthy and intricate to relate in this chapter. The focus herein is directed toward how you can navigate the bureaucratic waters in an effort to get paid for your services to the elder population.

For geriatric group work, Medicare is the major payer with some additional funding from private supplemental insurance policies or Medicaid. This is the typical funding process as long as the type of group work you provide meets Medicare guidelines and group leaders are appropriately licensed to render those services. Otherwise, you need to seek alternative funding sources, as presented in Chapter 14.

Currently, the impact shows that Medicare fee cuts have a reverse scalpel effect, cutting deepest into the fees of thoracic surgeons, radiologists, pathologists, and anesthesiologists (Moon, 1993). The big winners are family practice and general practice physicians, with an increase in payment of 27%–28%. Psychiatry anticipates a modest 3% payment gain (Health Care Financing Administration, 1991).

APPROVED PROVIDERS FOR GROUP WORK

Since the Omnibus Budget Reconciliation Act of 1989, Medicare Part B offers expanded coverage for clinical psychologists and licensed clinical social workers as independent providers without regard to place of service or in community mental health centers. Group providers may include these professionals as well as other qualified personnel under supervision by the approved providers while working as coleaders on-site. The Medicare Part B Update for your area will specify which licensed professionals in your state are qualified providers or stipulate qualifications for recognizing providers in states without license laws for psychology or social work (Inlander & MacKay, 1989).

Medicare numbers are issued to each qualified provider as well as to group providers. Group providers are required to list and update the names and individual numbers of providers working in the group. The group provider number is used for the billing of geriatric group work in a program like GSE.

Services are billed according to most current acceptable CPT (current procedural terminology) codes. Watch your Medicare Part B Update for any changes. When GSE groups began, the leaders were instructed at the provider seminar to bill H5020 for group therapy per hour. Shortly thereafter, the acceptable code changed to 90853. Our billing service discovered the change quickly. If you are doing your own billing, read the Update for any future changes. Medicare, Medicaid, and Medigap coverages also require a diagnosis code for each patient according to the current edition of *International Statistical Classification of Diseases* (World Health Organization, 1992).

SPEAKING THE MEDICARE LANGUAGE

Before entering the Medicare maze, you need to be able to translate and communicate in their highly refined jargon. Learn these key terms:

AAPCC = average annual per capita cost
Accept Assignment = treat the patient, then direct-bill Medicare
Allowed or Reasonable Charges = based on recent Medicare Fee Schedule
or, simply, what Medicare deems is the correct charge for services
Carriers = deal with Part B coverage
COLA = cost-of-living adjustment

Copayment = portion of costs for health services that is paid by the recipient

Custodial or sheltered care = nonmedical care

DME = durable medical equipment, suitable for prescribed ongoing use such as a wheelchair or a hospital bed

DRG = diagnosis-related group based on averages among hospital for treating a similar condition

Eligible recipients = persons age 65 and over, persons declared permanently and totally disabled, and persons with end-stage renal disease

EOMB = explanation of Medicare benefits, sent to the patient

ESRD = end-stage renal disease

HCFA = Health Care Financing Administration, a division of the U.S. Department of Health and Human Services, which oversees Medicare

HHA = home health agency

HI = hospital insurance under Part A

HMOs = Health maintenance organizations; offer Medicare alternative plans and receive some reimbursement from Medicare based on AAPCC

ICF = intermediate care facilities, a less intensive level of care than a skilled nursing facility

Intermediaries = deal with Part A coverage

MAAC = maximum allowable actual charge

MCCA = Medicare Catastrophic Coverage Act of 1988

Participating Providers = designated by Medicare on the basis of an agreement to accept assignment and bill directly

Medigap = supplemental insurance to cover costs of some or all deductibles and copayments

Medigap crossover = to simplify claims for a patient, the name, address, and policy number of any Medigap supplemental insurance is recorded by the provider or billing agent on the HCFA claim form in the box titled "other health insurance coverage"

MFS = Medicare Fee Schedule

Part A = hospital coverage, skilled nursing facility benefit, and hospice care

Part B = pays portion of services from physicians, consultation, mental health providers, X-ray and radiation therapy, ambulance services, and physical and speech therapy

PCS = provider claim summary

PIP = periodic interim payments

PPS = prospective payment system

PRO = peer review organizations

PSRO = professional standard review organization

QMBs = qualified Medicare beneficiaries

RBRVS = resource-based relative value scale to define relative value units

RVU = relative value units that establish time and complexity of services

SMI = supplementary medical insurance under Part B

SNF = skilled nursing facility

URC = utilization review committee

VPS = volume performance standards that give incentives to lower the rate of growth in physician services with an inverse relation penalty

MEDICAID

Operating with both federal and state oversight, Medicaid can function as a supplemental coverage to Medicare for qualified beneficiaries who are financially needy. States have some latitude in making the rules that define eligible recipients and covered services. Each state has a designated governmental department to administer Medicaid and receive its share of federal funds. A person who is blind, aged, or disabled and meets qualifications for Supplemental Security Income (SSI) typically becomes eligible for Medicaid. A substantial portion of Medicaid beneficiaries are eligible under the provision for the medically needy.

Each state also determines the qualifications and application process for psychology and mental health professionals to become providers. Some states seek to control costs by limiting the number of providers approved to render Medicaid-reimbursed services. To become a Medicaid provider for geriatric group services, contact your local Medicaid office or the state welfare and social services division to request a provider application. If you are accepted as a provider, you will receive the state provider manual, fee schedules, and billing directions. Guiding you through the paperwork and rules for Medicaid is another way in which a billing service is valuable to new providers.

BRIDGING THE MEDIGAP

At the time of enrollment into a group program, you need to obtain a copy of the patient's Medigap insurance card. Copy both sides! Be certain that the number, address, policy number, and claims information phone number are readable. Next, get the signature of the beneficiary (patient) in Blocks 12 and 13 of the HCFA form authorizing transmission of claim information and assignment of benefits to the provider. If the beneficiary does not handle his or her business matters, then the appropriate legal agent (family, guardian, or trustee) signs. At least one completed form must have a signature before you casually enter "signature on file."

Call or write your area Medicare representative to request the Specialty Update on Medicare Part B, for use by physicians and suppliers. This publication gives an alphabetical listing of Medigap supplemental insurers and their insurance code numbers.

MEDIGAP MEETS MANAGED CARE

The proliferation of managed care is increasingly evident in the supplemental coverages and HMOs. The effect of managed-care Medigap may be less restrictive than managed care for persons of younger ages who do not have the Medicare safety net. What managed care brings to Medigap is part of its overall trends toward (a) cost containment by limiting services, (b) controlling the length of treatment and methods used by providers, (c) requiring greater accountability and outcome measures, (d) emphasizing outpatient and least restrictive treatment options, and (e) encouraging group work. Notice that last point: group work. Managed care providers who are receptive to group work in younger populations are discovering the efficacy of this approach for elders. Here's where a smart geriatric group leader takes time to educate a Medigap managed-care case manager about the treatment approach and goals of geriatric groups as was done with the facility or patient's family. You need to emphasize the benefits, cost efficiency, and treatment efficacy of geriatric group therapy. Back up this claim with your own experience or with research and reports from comparable programs.

Medigap coverage delivered through managed care is just another type of supplemental coverage. Don't panic or run for cover. If your geriatric group program meets Medicare guidelines for payment, you have a strong potential to receive reimbursement from the supplemental policy.

ELECTRONIC BILLING: DO IT YOURSELF OR SUBCONTRACT?

Computerized transmission of billing to Medicare is expected. Service providers have two realistic choices: Do it yourself or hire a billing agent. Larger practices with multiple providers sharing the costs of billing and support services may benefit from in-house billing. Smaller providers probably will not. The computer equipment and software are expensive, require a knowledgeable operator, and are subject to breakdown. Only busy offices can afford a full backup on equipment and trained personnel. The problem of retaining trained billing personnel is the real disaster. Computers and software can be swiftly replaced. Billing clerks quit without warning or call in sick on critical data entry days. Hiring or training another person who can take over the operation without a costly interruption in billings and collections is a fantasy not often fulfilled. This is a particularly intense problem in offices with only one designated billing clerk.

After analyzing the costs and potential problems, GSE rejected the idea of in-house billing and interviewed billing services. With a comprehensive search, a variety of companies were identified in the area that offered full billing service for an average of 7%–9% on collected fees. This was an excellent deal considering the size of GSE group programs and a commitment to maintain low overhead. Medicare offers a "Vendor and Service Bureau Listing" that is extremely helpful. After searching the names of billing services in the area, the GSE leaders began to interview each candidate. The actual services were similar and the fees within a close range. What influenced the decision was the business owner's prior experience in billing for hospitals and insurers as well as an established track record in dealing with Medicare, Medicaid, and Medigap. They were further impressed by the training programs for personnel, their high percentage collection rate, and the detailed reports generated monthly for each client.

Effective billing is more than technology. Choose a billing service on the basis of expertise, adequate personnel, and verified performance for current clients. Location is another issue. Will claims be delivered or mailed to their office? The company GSE chose provided a pick-up service for claims on a weekly basis at no extra charge. Remember, you are in the business of providing group services. Any activity that takes you away from your primary work is money out of your pocket. A good billing agent works to keep you doing therapy instead of being in therapy by providing a user-friendly, turnkey service.

CHRONIC BILLING FATIGUE

Keep a close watch on Medicare EOMBs. Errors capriciously emerge and require mountain-moving efforts to correct. For example, one frustrating and expensive problem involved a rash of payment denials suddenly occurring for patients for whom payment had been made without interruption for several months. The capable billing service attempted all the usually effective strategies: rebilling, writing letters to request reconsideration, and telephone conferences with Blue Cross/Blue Shield in Jacksonville (which handles Florida Medicare claims). To make matters worse, the patients' EOMBs continued to read "not a covered service." That caused a guardian to remove two newer patients from our groups because he mistakenly thought there was something improper with Medicare reimbursement for group psychotherapy.

The situation became so frustrating and financially painful over several months that the billing agent felt personally challenged to locate the error. Here's where a highly experienced billing representative (not just a secretary who can type claims forms) makes all the difference. She insisted that the Medicare supervisor work with her to trace the path of the claims from the time received by electronic transfer all the way through the maze to payment. The billing agent, not the supervisor, found an input error at Medicare in which GSE's provider code was inaccurately typed and the facility was coded as a provider of durable medical equipment.

After writing a letter of explanation to patients and their families, guardians, or trustees, the crisis was over. Did Medicare apologize for the error occurred in their internal systems or expedite the overdue payments? No. GSE did finally collect checks over the summer for services rendered during the first quarter of the year.

The point of this story is that if you have a chronic problem collecting reimbursement, bring in a consultant or other expert who has a highly analytical mind, computer wizardry, and the persistence to leap over all the bureaucratic roadblocks.

HOW TO CONSISTENTLY GET PAID

Experience is a treacherous yet terrific teacher. So that you may avoid replaying some of GSE's lessons, here is how to avoid some expensive hurdles and improve your payment record with Medicare and supplements:

1   Attend a regional Medicare provider seminar. In addition to your lecture notes, you finish the day with a collection of booklets and other vital paperwork. You also meet people from the regional Medicare office whom you may need to contact in the future. For new providers, this is worth your time.

2   Don't submit a single form until you understand all blanks, boxes, and lines.

3   Keep copies of everything sent to Medicare!

4   Document all treatment contacts, methods, and results. The rule is if you can't prove it, don't bill for it.

5   Coordinate with the facility's treatment plan. This is additional justification for your work if questioned.

6   If the location of your groups does not maintain treatment plans (as nursing homes do), maintain and update a treatment plan for each group member. Good treatment planning and good billing procedures are mutually supportive.

7   Set up a random-check procedure for all claims generated in your office. Assign a person who does not regularly input the claims to proofread and random-check them. Do this weekly for at least 3 months until things are running smoothly. Thereafter, extend the checkups to bimonthly and without notice.

8   If you use a billing service, ask about their procedure for random checking.

9   Set up account codes for Medicare receivables and reimbursements that are different from any other income in your office. You need to have a clear picture of the revenue generated from group work for business and tax planning.

10   Establish a tickler system with calendar, notes, or computer software that flags overdue payments from Medicare.

11   Don't let more than 3 months pass before making a major effort to get paid on claims submitted. Whether you resubmit or request tracking, be pleasantly persistent.

12   Read all Medicare Update bulletins within 48 hours of arrival in your mailbox! New information that affects your payments is printed there, and you, as a provider, are expected to read it and follow any new procedures.

Finally, getting paid for geriatric group work under Medicare is not substantially more or less difficult than dealing with many other third-party payers in this increasingly provider-restrictive, managed-care world. The greatest irritations are in setting up the program and tracking periodic problems. Beyond that, you can return to the more exciting business of providing innovative, interactive geriatric group therapy to patients whose lives are enriched by your work.

Chapter 14

Alternative Funding for Elder Groups

A business with an income at its heels, furnishes always oil for its own wheels.

—William Cowper, *Retirement* (1782)

Bringing your own basket to a class reunion picnic is one thing, but finding your own funding for group work? Yes, it's possible and becoming an enticing option for four basic reasons:

1   Not all group leaders who are suitable for certain types of group work qualify as Medicare providers.

2   Services covered today under Medicare, Medicaid, and Medigap may be reduced or eliminated tomorrow.

3   Cost-containment efforts may limit types of group work to brief psychotherapy for major depression or other severe diagnostic categories and refuse to pay for creative modalities that deal with adjustment, pain, life span crises, and grief.

4   The oncoming tidal wave of baby boomers into retirement means that early in the 21st century there will be far more geriatric patients in need of service than money to pay for those services, according even to optimistic estimates of the Medicare and Medicaid systems.

The ideas that follow are to motivate you to discover opportunities for developing a geriatric group program. In so doing, group leaders become partners with significant elements of the local community in the delivery of elder services.

NONPROFIT ORGANIZATIONS

The most visible nonprofit local service organizations are churches, community centers, and senior citizen centers. Look over the bulletins of several large local churches, and a senior adult program or ministry is usually found. Many community centers plan social, recreational, and exercise activities for senior adults during the midday hours when their other populations, working adults and children, are not prime users of the facility. Naturally, senior citizen centers are targeted to meet a full spectrum of needs for elders.

Geriatric group programs can be tailored to fit the needs of participants in any of these existing organizations. Elders are already attracted to these facilities, so there is some built-in potential for group membership. These organizations have a loyal membership, identity in the community, methods of promoting their programs (i.e., bulletins, newsletters, etc.), multipurpose building space, and other valuable community connections. A well-planned, multimodal geriatric group brings a fresh approach to a schedule that is often filled with traditional arts and crafts or coffee clubs. Don't be shy about reminding the center director that geriatric groups can generate new interest in the overall program by offering something that meets an immediate need. Short-term grief groups, particularly near holidays, may motivate newcomers to attend for this purpose and discover that there are other activities at the center that they may attend. This is a win–win situation: The elders win by finding new opportunities to socialize and learn, and the center wins with greater usage and the potential to gain new members.

The group program might be designed with two tracks: a closed group series for 5 weeks on art and expression or phototherapy and several alternating open groups. Many community centers have a season or semester calendar similar to school with fall, winter, spring, and summer sessions. Plan programs accordingly.

Set a minimum enrollment number for closed groups and prepare adequate materials. As part of the nonprofit organization's program schedule, geriatric groups gain an implied endorsement of that organization, so be certain you want to share their reputation and population.

RESEARCH GRANTS

Grants are waiting for the taking, grants are impossible to get—which depends on who responds. The bigger the bucks, the tougher the competition. Fortunately, that's not a major issue for the geriatric group program. You don't need millions; you need thousands. Attracting the interest of multinational corporations and national agencies is less significant than finding support from regional corporations and state agencies. Think medium to small. Search for supplemental funding for local geriatric group work, not a full staff and a limo.

The fine art of grant seeking and writing is the subject of many books and too extensive to include here. Begin by investing in attending a weekend seminar or local evening college course on grant writing. Next, talk with local community centers, senior centers, or area offices on aging about the group leaders' desire to find additional support for geriatric groups as well as contribute to research in the field.

Find the nearest university with a graduate program in gerontology, counseling, or social work. Universities are virtual heat-seeking missiles for grants. So what do you have to offer them? Geriatric groups are another training site for students as coleaders or assistants.

Spend time in the library or on Internet sources scouting notices and directories of grants. Look for such titles as *elderly health services, gerontology and mental health*, or *social services*. Several grant directories are listed in the resources at the end of this book.

Before deciding to pursue larger research grants, be certain that you have the desire and ability to produce a quality study that will genuinely enhance the profession of gerontology. Grants are not the answer to support an otherwise ineffective and unsuccessful geriatric program.

COMMUNITY GRANTS

Making the city, county, and area a better place to live is everybody's business, particularly key employers'. The trend toward visibly investing back into the local area is catching on in corporations of all sizes. From the pledge to clean up a highway mile to sponsorship of wheelchair sporting events, local companies are following the corporate giants in doing good works.

Ask the larger local and regional corporations if they have any minigrants for investment in specialized programs to serve their community. Corporations may, particularly if they profit from offering products to elders, want the positive image of supporting a community elder service. Civic and service clubs underwrite various local projects. If you are primarily seeking scholarship money for elders who cannot afford to attend geriatric groups in a community setting, then several smaller grants may be sufficient.

ADULT DAY-CARE

Elders are living longer at a time when custodial care costs are skyrocketing. Moving in with adult children or other family members is one choice that reduces expenses but leaves the elder at home alone during the day while younger adults are at work. Filling the gap in care for these elders is adult day-care. To make this care feasible for working adult children, many elder day-cares open early and close late to conform to work hours, much as does children's day-care.

Like their youthful counterparts, elders may spend up to 10 hours in adult day-care. Meaningful activity is important during these most productive hours of an elder's day. With many blocks of time to fill, multimodal geriatric groups are a welcome alternative for the participants and the weary staff. Further ideas for including group work under contract to the day-care are presented in the next section on fees. Adult day-care is more advanced in some areas than others. Visit or write to these programs in other cities to inquire about their daily schedules. This practical research gives you ideas about the types of groups that are presently working well in other adult day-cares. Demonstrate your knowledge of this subject and your plan for geriatric group work when you present your concept to an adult day-care director.

DETERMINING YOUR FEES

Many group leaders have difficulty asking for payment. Persons who choose the helping professions are notoriously reluctant collection agents. However, meeting the needs in the largely underserved elder population won't happen unless group leaders get paid for their work.

Group leaders who are appropriately licensed and qualify as Medicare providers have payment guidelines to use in setting fees. Seriously consider what fees are realistic. Otherwise, set fees for group that are reasonable within your community, based on an informal survey of prices. There is a financial advantage in working with nonprofit organizations or adult day-care. The greater latitude given to use an organization's facility and its promotional publications, the less overhead and expenses for the group.

Many community recreation centers have other fee-based programs such as genealogy, woodworking, and breakfast club. Their members are accustomed to paying to participate. Geriatric group fees can be slightly higher yet within a reasonable range, based on what types of groups are offered. Closed groups with more focus and preparation of the activities command higher per-group (or session) fees than open groups. Certain types of closed groups work best with a smaller group, or you can add a coleader. A closed-group fee may range from $10–$15 per person at each session compared with $5–$10 per person for open-group sessions. Without the Medicare limit on group size, a well-trained leader can, for example, manage a dozen people in a bibliotherapy or humor group. Even at the lower open-group fees, that's $60 to $120 hourly with almost no overhead expenses.

For any church that shows interest in its senior adults, geriatric groups are a natural extension of outreach to elders. The easiest way to begin is to schedule groups within or adjacent to an existing church senior adult program. Many churches have a full weekday morning of activities that occurs weekly or biweekly. Another way to make the session more open to all interested seniors is to recommend that the church offer some scholarship or underwriting assistance for members to attend your groups. The church may decide to approve financial aid requests and determine whether to match funds or make full payment for needy elder members—another win–win situation. Geriatric groups enhance the senior adult ministry, and the church assists in payment for disadvantaged elders to participate.

Senior citizen centers and adult day-care are fully dedicated to elders, so every day demands an agenda of stimulating activities, like a GSE-style geriatric group program! Talk with the director to learn about his or her needs. You may also discover that the senior center has several funding sources from donations, cities, clubs, and other community support. As with churches, the senior centers may have access to funds to underwrite participation in group for some needy elders. Emphasize the ease of offering groups as an activities fee option or for the center to contract for groups for all participants.

Considering the lengthy hours of operation for many adult day-care centers, multimodal geriatric groups are a productive addition to long hours for elders away from their homes. Remind the day-care director that elders who are involved in satisfying pursuits, discovering things about themselves and finding appreciative outlets for their reminiscences, complain far less and are more cooperative. Payment in this scenario is a type of contract work between the day-care and your geriatric group program to deliver a certain number of groups or for a stated amount of time. Be careful about accepting a per-client, per-group fee only, or other performance-oriented fees. Set a fee by the type of service rendered and for a maximum number of participants. For example, a leader may charge $60 per group hour to conduct remotivation group for up to 10 participants, three times weekly. The fee can be slightly less per group hour if contracted for more than 5 hours weekly. Whatever financial incentives are offered, pay is better for staying 4 hours at one location than for working 2 hours at two locations with unpaid travel time between sites.

INCOME TAX CONSIDERATIONS

Are you an independent contractor just because you have a contract with a center to provide geriatric group work? The answer is maybe. The way to determine the accurate answer to the satisfaction of the Internal Revenue Service is to pass the "Twenty Factors Test" found in IRS Publication 937, *Employment Taxes and Information Returns*. Scoring 100% means you are an independent contractor. Missing even 1 out of 20 classifies you as an employee. Remaining an independent contractor can be in both your best interest and that of the organization where you conduct groups. Failure to meet this test can deem you an employee of the organization. Consult the IRS publication for details and discuss any questions with a tax accountant or certified public accountant.

SURVIVAL OF THE CREATIVE

In the evolution of health care, the need for geriatric services is rising at a time when costs are being trimmed. Case managers are making dozens of critical care decisions daily. Is group therapy for an elder this week more important than funds that may be needed next month for that same person's hospitalization? That's a difficult and circuitous question. Yet it's the kind of question about financially limited resources that exists in managed health care and increasingly in Medicare and Medicaid.

If nothing else is learned from reading this chapter, please grasp the concept that being creative in seeking funding sources and contract work opportunities for geriatric groups is a viable alternative. Take a consultation approach and find a capable business planner or an informal group of local businesspeople who will give advice on carrying out ideas in this chapter. Working with the local Small Business Association center is another way to expand business knowledge. Take advantage of a wealth of business information and local seminars provided by the U.S. Small Business Association, a government service. Look in your phone directory for a listing or call 1-800-827-5722 (within the continental United States).

No matter what happens with insurance and Medicare funding, the need for geriatric groups is growing as the population ages. Geriatric group programs that have mastered the art of finding creative funding alternatives will survive and blossom in the approaching era of tight third-party purse strings.

Chapter 15

Looking Ahead: The Future of Geriatric Group Work

Working with elder groups is a grand adventure in the emerging multidisciplinary approach to gerontology. Every geriatric group leader is a pioneer searching for new and better techniques to reach, restore, and revitalize a growing elder population. In 1996, the first wave of baby boomers in the United States turned 50 and became eligible for a discount on coffee, among other privileges of maturity. Following them is a veritable tsunami of baby boomers who are expected to live longer and make greater demands on mental health services during their retirement years.

TEN TARGETS FOR THE 21ST CENTURY

Within this oncoming new generation of elders are additional challenges for geriatric group programs. Group leaders and other elder care providers must seize this window of opportunity to be prepared for the future shock of changes. The next generation of service delivery for the elder population will be both altered and enhanced by these 10 target areas.

Target 1: Increased Involvement with Managed Care

A delicate balance will eventually be reached between the post–World War II overutilization of medical services and the underutilization incentives of managed care's infancy. Once split, the atom could not be called back. Likewise, the unleashing of cost containment is a factor in planning future geriatric services. Fortunately, managed care systems are generally supportive of group programs.

The persistent problems that annually threaten both Medicare and Medicaid may drive these government-run systems into the waiting arms of managed care. Regardless of the final product, it is not now politically correct to deny basic services for senior adults. Try changing that scenario in the face of the large number of politically savvy, willing-to-protest baby boomers turning seniors. The issue for geriatric group providers is to become a significant part of the managed care treatment team.

What can be done? Don't just request group services and assume that approval follows. With each request or initial contracting, send a concise package presenting group services. In a single-page cover letter, state the program goal and how that goal serves the managed care system clients. Add two to four pages with a sample format or schedule, short biographies of group leaders, and letters or excerpted comments from facility administrators, nursing supervisors, or physicians attesting to the value of your services.

Every time a group leader or therapist successfully "sells" the value of geriatric group programs to a major managed care system, the door opens wider for others to follow. The program benefits and so do the clients.

Target 2: More Interaction
with Geriatric-Sensitive Medical Providers

Although managed care systems create a higher demand for general practice physicians, there are complementary opportunities for those who have geriatric training. Medicine and counseling are racing to measure up with nursing, which has a longer tradition of geriatric care training.

Geriatric group program leaders need to make their services known to primary care physicians, nurse practitioners, physician's assistants, nurses, physical therapists, home health case managers, and local hospice services. Get on the team! Or if there is not a collegial atmosphere in the local area, start by organizing informal breakfast meetings or continuing education.

Target 3: Greater Emphasis on Assessment

Efforts to convince all medical and mental health providers that aging is not a disorder are still critical. Proper medical and psychological assessment as well as determination of readiness for group participation are as necessary for elders as for those at any other age. All group leaders—whether activity directors, social services workers, nurses, or psychologists—need to establish standards for intake, assessment, evaluation, and follow-up that are suitable to every group and the training of the leader. Managed care systems demand such standards for reimbursement. To give less is unacceptable, regardless of payment mode.

Group leaders who are professionally qualified to use psychological testing need to regularly scan the gerontology journals for the implementation, research, and practical value of current and new instruments. Of particular concern in the future will be the availability of updated norms or redesigned instruments appropriate for multicultural elder populations and more defined age categories (for example, the 60- to 69-year-old young-old compared with the 80+ very old).

Target 4: Adaptation of Brief Therapy Techniques

The Freudian couch and other symbols of therapy as a lifelong adventure are dinosaurs in an era of shorter term, focused, solution-oriented therapy. Efficacy and economics herald the reign of brief therapy that is likely to continue well into the next century of counseling. Now is the time for trend-smart group leaders to learn brief therapy techniques and determine how these techniques apply to geriatric group programs.

Essential principles of brief therapy are highly compatible to working with elders, specifically, believing in the resourcefulness of clients, focusing attention on positives, finding satisfaction in small changes, and respecting clients' expertise about themselves (Walter & Peller, 1992). Brief therapy groups may constitute anywhere from 6 to 12 sessions or up to 26 weeks. The definition is fluid as long as the goals, format, and usefulness to the clients are reasonably justified.

Target 5: Multicultural Awareness

Air travel, electronic communications, international economic links, and a widespread ease of passage between most nations of the world seem to shrink the size of our planet. Whether living in the rural Midwest, Deep South, or metropolitan Northeast, American cities are more a banquet of races and cultures than the old concept of a melting pot. In this context, group leaders are challenged to understand the cultural influences, social norms, and gestures of respect that are appropriate for increasingly multicultural elder groups.

University sociology departments and local government urban planning offices can provide updated information on changes in cultural and racial demographics that are represented in the geographic area served by a geriatric group program. Read, attend lectures, and talk with other geriatric providers about how to best meet these changing needs.

Target 6: Programs for Inner City Elders and Homeless Elders

Without a miraculous solution in the next decade, the socially isolated inner city dwellers and homeless elders will remain an underserved population. Here's where basic skills and short-term groups may work best with an unattached population. As opportunities to serve these elders become available in urban community centers, food centers, or churches, group leaders have the task of adapting modalities to meet these needs. The task is awesome, and the needs are growing.

Target 7: Relationship Issues of Elder Couples

As men and women live longer past traditional retirement at age 65, so does their potential to sustain or develop romantic relationships. The adjustment to an empty nest and more time together is increasingly interrupted by adult children and grandchildren returning home following divorce, early widowhood, or economic crisis. Other elder couples are being torn apart by divorce, substance abuse, and suicide. Dating and mating are increasingly more popular than afternoon bridge games for single senior adults who desire another relationship. Group leaders have to be better prepared to deal with issues of sexuality, attraction, breakups, and commitment.

Target 8: Training in Elder Abuse and Domestic Violence

Physical, emotional, and sexual abuse may be the modern-day equivalent of bubonic plague in the devastation that is left behind for families and individuals. Sadly, so much abuse occurs among and against senior adults that many states have specific laws for mandatory reporting of elder abuse.

All geriatric group leaders, regardless of professional or lay status, need regular training in recognizing the signs of domestic violence, neglect, manipulation, or intimidation of elders. Perpetrators of elder abuse include spouses, adult children, relatives, and caregivers. Elder abuse can occur in private homes, assisted living facilities, nursing homes, or hospitals. Never assume that an elder living alone or with relatives is more or less at risk than one living in a long-term care facility.

Be aware of the state statute's definition of who is a "mandatory reporter" for suspected elder abuse. Can a report be made by telephone hotline or must it be presented in writing? Does every group leader know the procedure for reporting and how to document this action in the group program records? Group leaders have a responsibility to direct suspected abuse victims to local domestic violence shelters, crisis intake centers, the social service government agency with local jurisdiction, or the area nursing home ombudsman office.

Target 9: Counseling Readiness of 21st-Century Elders

Expect the aging baby boomer generation to be far more receptive to participation in elder groups than their parents' generation. These new elders came from 1960s-era communal living and encounter groups, and they view counseling as an acceptable, sometimes fashionable option for dealing with personal, relationship, and family problems. They have a longer history of being outspoken and seeking self-improvement. A significant number of these new elders have experience as members of support groups, substance abuse groups, and personal growth groups. Geriatric group leaders are likely to spend minimal time with the formative stages of group and have potential for more intense and productive working group stages. However, these group-wise elders come with more preconceived ideas of how groups function and what constitutes an effective leader.

Target 10: Opportunities
for the Practitioner-Researcher

Geriatric group work occurs in the field, not in the lab. Bringing services into the community, nursing home, or assisted care facility makes participation more feasible and gives an unmined wealth of data on elder groups. Even though many counseling and psychology graduates retain the belief that statistics evoke much stress, research is much more than number crunching. Thankfully, sophisticated computer programs take on much of that tedious task.

Think beyond thesis and dissertation topics. This is real group work with a significant population in which so much is yet to be learned. Share discoveries, theories, and ideas with other practitioners. Don't just attend geriatric conferences and soak up information. Be a conference presenter. Teach in-service training. Write articles or responses to other professional articles. Discuss ideas with researchers and seek their reactions. Too many good ideas are wasting away in group leaders' chart notes. This book is the result of sharing as a means of teaching, encouraging, and stimulating other group leaders to do more and do it better.

CONCLUDING OBSERVATIONS

The 10 targets for the 21st century are challenges for the future that can begin to be addressed in the present. Today's geriatric groups will have a significant impact on the direction of these services for 21st-century mental health systems. By now, the experienced group leaders and neophytes who find elder group work exciting are thinking about the preferred modalities or the ideas adaptable to their personal leadership style. That's the best possible response to display after being immersed in this short course on the Geriatric Skills Enhancement program.

This book was intended to be savored like a rich sandwich piled high with a favorite filling in the center (Part 2, Geriatric Skills Enhancement Modalities) and held together by those necessary, thick bread slices (Part 1, Group Techniques for Aging Populations, and Part 3, Financial Support for Elder Groups). The needs of specific elder groups, available facilities, and leaders' skills will determine how the reader develops and flavors a new group program or revises an existing treatment plan.

Group leaders, beware: This is fresh territory where dozens of theorists have not yet traveled. It's not as safe as another review of Freud or as predictable as a new verse for the familiar refrains on rational behavior. The road is not paved with shelves of books on the definitive methods. No, fellow group leaders, geriatric group work is waiting for the select, the capable, the creative, and the bold. Leaders who are defining the future of geriatric group work every day by meeting real needs of real people. Leaders like you!

References

Abraham, I. L. (1992). Longitudinal reliability of the life satisfaction index (short form) with nursing home residents: A cautionary note. *Perceptual and Motor Skills, 75*, 665–666.

Annual report of the Board of Trustees of the Hospital Insurance Trust Fund. (1981). Washington, DC: U.S. Government Printing Office

Birren, J. E. (1987). The best of all stories. *Psychology Today, 21*, 91–92.

Blau, Z. S. (1973). *Old age in a changing society.* New York: New Viewpoints.

Bledsoe, N., & Lutz-Ponder, P. (1986). Group counseling with nursing home residents. *Journal for Specialists in Group Work, 11*, 37–41.

Brink, T. L., Curran, P., Dorr, M. L., Janson, E., McNulty, U., & Messina, M. (1985). Geriatric Depression Scale reliability: Order, examiner and reminiscence effects. *Clinical Gerontologist, 3(4)*, 57–60.

Brink, T. L., Yesavage, J. A., Lum, O., Heersma, P., Adey, M., & Rose, T. L. (1982). Screening test for geriatric depression. *Clinical Gerontologist, 1*, 37–43.

Bryant, W. (1991). Creative group work with confused elderly people: A development of sensory integration therapy. *British Journal of Occupational Therapy, 54(5)*, 187–192.

Burlew, L. D., Jones, J., & Emerson, P. (1991). Exercise and the elderly: A group counseling approach. *The Journal for Specialists in Group Work, 16(3)*, 152–158.

Burnside, I. M. (1973). *Psychosocial nursing care of the aged.* New York: McGraw Hill.

Burnside, I. M., & Schmidt, M. G. (1984). *Working with older adults: Group process and techniques* (2nd ed.). Boston: Jones & Bartlett.

Burnside, I., & Schmidt, M. (1994). *Working with older adults: Group process and techniques* (3rd ed.). Boston: Jones & Bartlett.

Butler, R. N. (1963). The life review: An interpretation of reminiscence in the aged. *Psychiatry, 26*, 65–76.

Cohen, C. I. (1990). Psychotherapy with the elderly in public mental health settings. *New Directions for Mental Health Services, 46*, 81–92

Cohen, H. J., & Geussner, J. R. (1989). Comprehensive geriatric assessment: Mission not accomplished. *Journal of Gerontology, 44*, 175–77.

Cole, M. (1990). Ritual and therapy: Casting the circle of change. *Pratt Institute Creative Arts Therapy Review, 11*, 13–21.

Corey, G., & Corey, M. S. (1987). *Groups: Process and practice* (3rd ed.). Pacific Grove, CA: Brooks/Cole.

Cousins, N. (1979). *Anatomy of an illness.* New York: W. W. Norton & Co.

Clements, W. M. (1982). Therapeutic functions of recreation in reminiscence with aging persons. In M. L. Teague, R. D. MacWeil, & G. L. Hutzhuser (Eds.), *Perspectives on leisure and aging.* Columbia: University of Missouri.

Creanza, A. L., & McWhirter, J. J. (1994). Reminiscence: A strategy for getting to know you. *Journal for Specialists in Group Work, 19*(4), 232–237.

Crose, R. (1990). Reviewing the past in the here and now: Using Gestalt therapy techniques with life review. *Journal of Mental Health Counseling, 12*(3), 279–287.

Dewey, J. (1939). *Theory of valuation.* Chicago: University of Chicago Press.

Dimmer, S. A., Carroll, J. L., & Wyatt, G. K. (1990). Uses of humor in psychotherapy. *Psychological Reports, 66,* 795–801.

Docherty, F. (1986). Community programs for the depressed elderly. *Physical and Occupational Therapy in Geriatrics, 5,* 59–76.

Edinberg, M. (1985). *Mental health practice with the elderly.* Englewood Cliffs, NJ: Prentice Hall.

Erlanger, M. A. (1990). Using the genogram with the older client. *Journal of Mental Health Counseling, 12*(3), 321–330.

Erwin, K. T. (1992). *Interactive, multi-modal group therapy for aging adults.* Paper presented at the American Association for Counseling and Development National Conference, Baltimore.

Erwin, K. (1993). Looking backward, looking ahead—Helping elders cope. *Christian Counseling Today, 1*(3), 33–36.

Ewers, M., Jacobson, S., Powers, V., & McConney, P. (1983). *Humor, the tonic you can afford: A handbook of ways of using humor in long term care.* Los Angeles: Ethel Percy Andrus Gerontological Center.

Feder, J. M. (1977). *Medicare: The politics of federal hospital insurance.* Lexington, MA: Lexington Books.

Folsom, J. (1968). Reality orientation for the elderly mental patient. *Journal of Geriatric Psychiatry, 1,* 291–307.

Folstein, M. F., Folstein, S. E., & McHugh, P. R. (1975). Mini-Mental State: A practical method for grading the cognitive state of patients for the clinician. *Journal of Psychiatric Research, 12,* 189–198.

Forsythe, E. (1989). One to one therapeutic recreation activities for the bed and/or room bound. *Activities, Adaptation and Aging, 13,* 63–76.

Freud, S. (1960). *Jokes and their relation to the unconscious.* New York: W. W. Norton.

Glasgow, R. E., & Rosen, G. M. (1978). Behavioral bibliotherapy: A review of self-help behavior therapy manuals. *Psychological Bulletin, 85,* 1–23.

Glasser, W. (1965). *Reality therapy: A new approach to psychiatry.* New York: Harper & Row.

Grimm, D. W. (1994). Therapist spiritual and religious values in psychotherapy. *Counseling and Values, 38*(3), 154–164.

Hanser, S. B. (1988). Controversy in music listening and stress reduction research. *Arts Psychotherapy, 15,* 211–217.

Harlan, J. E. (1990). The use of art therapy for older adults with developmental disabilities. *Activities, Adaptation and Aging, 15,* 67–79.

Harlan, J. E. (1993). The therapeutic value of art for persons with Alzheimer's disease and related disorders. *Loss, Grief and Care, 6,* 99–106.

Harrison, C. L. (1980). Therapeutic art programs around the world. *American Journal of Art Therapy, 19,* 99–101.

Hately, B. (1985). Spiritual well-being through life histories. *Journal of Religion and Aging, 1*(2), 63–71.

Havinghurst, R. J., & Glasser, A. (1972). An exploratory study of reminiscence. *Journal of Gerontology, 27,* 245–253.

Health Care Financing Administration. (1991). *Program statistics: Medicare and Medicaid data book.* Washington, DC: Author.

Hern, B. G., & Weis, D. M. (1991). A group counseling experience with the very old. *Journal for Specialists in Group Work, 16,* 143–151.

Hughes, M. (1995). *Bereavement and support: Healing in a healthy group environment.* Washington, DC: Taylor & Francis.

Hynes, A. M., & Wedl, L. C. (1990). *Bibliotherapy: An interactive process in counseling older persons.* Journal of Mental Health Counseling, 12(3), 288–302.

Ingersoll, B., & Silverman, A. (1978). Comparative group psychotherapy for the aged, *The Gerontologist, 18*(2), 201–206.

Inlander, C. B., & MacKay, C. K. (1989). *Medicare made easy.* Reading, MA: Addison-Wesley.

Johnson, C., Lahey, P., & Shore, A. (1992). An exploration of creative arts therapeutic group work on an Alzheimer's unit. *Arts in Psychotherapy, 19*(4), 269–277.

Joyce, T. A., & Taylor, V. L. (1990). Mastering words and managing conversations; therapy as dialogue. *Journal of Strategic and Systemic Therapies, 9*(4), 21–28.

Kaminsky, M. (1975). *What's inside you shines out of you.* New York: Horizon Press.

Kaminsky, M. (1984). *The uses of reminiscence: New ways of working with older adults.* New York: Haworth Press.

Katz, S. L. (1987). Photocollage as a therapeutic modality for working with groups. *Social Work with Groups, 10*(4), 83–90.

Kennedy, L. (1991). Humor in group psychotherapy. *Group, 15*(4), 234–241.

Koch, K. (1977). *I never told anybody: Teaching poetry writing in the nursing home.* New York: Random House.

Kohlberg, L. (1963). The development of children's orientation toward a moral order: Sequence in the development of moral thought. *Vita Humana, 6,* 11–35.

Kozma, A., & Stones, M. J. (1980). The measurement of happiness development of the Memorial University of Newfoundland Scale of Happiness (MUNSH). *The Journal of Gerontology, 35,* 906–912.

Lazarus, A. A. (1976). Multimodal behavior therapy. In C. M. Franks (Series Ed.), *Springer series in behavior modification: Vol. 1.* New York: Springer.

Lederman, S. (1988). *Humor: A tool for the psychoanalyst. Issues in Ego Psychology, 11*(2), 55–59.

Leszcz, M. (1990). Towards an integrated model of group psychotherapy with the elderly. *International Journal of Group Psychotherapy, 40,* 379–399.

Lewis, C. N. (1970). Reminiscing and self concept in old age. *Journal of Gerontology, 26,* 240–243.

Lewis, G. L. (1979). Adler's theory of personality and art therapy in a nursing home. *Art Psychotherapy, 6,* 47–50.

Lewis, M., & Butler, R. N. (1974). Life review therapy: Putting memories to work in individual and group psychotherapy. *Geriatrics, 29,* 1304–1305.

Lindeman, D. A., Downing, R., Corby, N. H., & Sanborn, B. (1991). *Alzheimer's day care: A basic guide.* New York: Hemisphere.

LoGerfo, M. (1980-81). Three ways of reminiscence in theory and practice. *International Journal of Aging & Human Development, 12*(1), 39–48.

Lowenthal, R. I., & Marrazzo, R. A. (1990). Milestoning: Evoking memories for resocialization through group reminiscence. *The Gerontologist, 30,* 269–272.

Lusterman, D. D. (1992). Humor as metaphor. *Psychotherapy in Private Practice, 10,* 167–172.

MacHovec, F. (1991). Humor in therapy. *Psychotherapy in Private Practice, 9,* 25–33.

Maloney, C., & Daily, T. (1986). An eclectic group program for nursing home residents with dementia. *Physical and Occupational Therapy in Geriatrics, 4,* 55–80.

Maslow, A. H. (1959). *New knowledge in human values.* New York: Harper & Brothers.

McGoldrick, M., & Gerson, R. (1985). *Genograms in family assessment.* New York: W. W. Norton.

McGuire, F. A., Boyo, R., & James, A. (1992). *Therapeutic humor with the elderly.* New York: Haworth Press.

McKinley, F. (1977). Exploration in bibliotherapy. *Personnel and Guidance Journal, 56,* 550–552.

McMurray, J. (1989). Creative arts with older people. *Activities, Adaptation and Aging, 14,* 1–138.

Meacham, J. A. (1995). Reminiscing as a process of social construction. In B. K. Haight & J. D. Webster (Eds.), *The art and science of reminiscing* (pp. 37–48). Washington, DC: Taylor & Francis.

Merriam, S. (1989). The structure of simple reminiscence. *Gerontologist, 29*(6), 761–767.

Meyerhoff, B., & Tufte, V. (1975). Life history as integration: An essay on an experiential model. *The Gerontologist, 15,* 541–543.

Moberg, P. J., & Lazarus, L. W. (1990). Psychotherapy of depression in the elderly. *Psychiatric Annals, 20,* 92–96.

Moon, M. (1993). *Medicare now and then.* Washington, DC: The Urban Institute Press.

Murphy, M. C., Conley, J., & Hernandez, M. A. (1994). Group remotivation therapy for the 90's. *Perspectives in Psychiatric Care, 30*, 9–12.

National Institutes of Health. (1991). Diagnosis and treatment of depression in late life. *Consensus statement* (pp. 8–9). Bethesda, MD: Author.

National Institutes of Health consensus statement: The National Institutes of Health consensus development conference statement. (1988). *Journal of American Geriatric Society, 36*, 342–347.

Neugarten, B. L., Havighurst, R. J., & Tobin, S. S. (1961). The measurement of life satisfaction. *Journal of Gerontology, 16*, 134–143.

Parmalee, P. A., & Katz, I. R. (1990). Geriatric Depression Scale. *Journal of the American Geriatrics Society, 38*, 1379.

Parmalee, P. A., Katz, I. R., & Lawton, M. P. (1989). Depression among institutionalized aged. *Journal of Gerontology, 44*, M-29.

Peter, L., & Dana, B. (1982). *The laughter prescription.* New York: Ballantine.

Piaget, J. (1965). *The moral judgment of the child* (M. Gabin, trans.). New York: Free Press. (Original published 1932)

Potenza, M., & Labbancz, M. (1989). The use of poetry in a day care center for Alzheimer's disease. *American Journal of Alzheimer's Care and Related Disorders & Research, 10*–12.

Prest, L. A., & Keller, J. F. (1993). Spirituality and family therapy; spiritual beliefs, myths, and metaphors. *Journal of Marital and Family Therapy, 19*(2), 137–148.

Raths, L., Hamin, M., & Simon, S. (1966). *Values and teaching: Working with values in the classroom.* Columbus, OH: Charles E. Merrill.

Reed, P. G. (1991). Spirituality and mental health in older adults: Extant knowledge for nursing. *Family and Community Health, 14*(2), 14–25.

Robinson, A. M. (no date). *Remotivation techniques: A manual for use in nursing homes.* Philadelphia: American Psychiatric Association/Smith, Kline & French Laboratories Remotivation Project.

Rogers, C. R. (1961). *On becoming a person.* Boston: Houghton Mifflin.

Rutherford, K. (1994). Humor in psychotherapy. *Individual Psychology Journal of Adlerian Theory, 50*, 207–222.

Salamon, M. J., & Conte, V. A. (1984). *The Life Satisfaction in the Elderly Scale.* Odessa, FL: Psychological Assessment Resources.

Satow, R. (1991). Three perspectives on humor and laughing: Classical, object relations and self psychology. *Group, 15*(4), 242–245.

Schnarch, D. M. (1990). Therapeutic uses of humor in psychotherapy. *Journal of Family Psychotherapy, 1*, 75–86.

Schrank, F., & Engels, D. (1981). Bibliotherapy as a counseling adjunct: Research findings. *The Personnel and Guidance Journal, 60*, 143–147.

Scogin, F., Hamblin, D., & Beutler, L. (1987). Bibliotherapy for depressed older adults: A self-help alternative. *The Gerontologist, 27*(3), 383–387.

Sherman, S., & Havinghurst, R. J. (1970). An exploratory study of reminiscence. *The Gerontologist, 10*, 42.

Sonstroem, R. J., & Morgan, W. P. (1989). Exercise and self-esteem: Rationale and model. *Medicine and Science in Sports and Exercise, 21*, 329–337.

Stewart, D. (1979). Phototherapy: theory and practice. *Art Psychotherapy, 6*(1), 41–46.

Stoedefalke, K. G. (1985). Motivating and sustaining the older adult in an exercise program. *Topics in Geriatric Rehabilitation, 1*, 78–86.

Sue, D. W., & Sue, D. (1990). *Counseling the culturally different.* New York: John Wiley & Sons.

Sweeney, T. J. (1990). Early recollections: A promising technique for use with older people. *Journal of Mental Health Counseling, 12*(3), 260–269.

Swenson, A. B. (1991). Relationships: Art education, art therapy, and special education. *Perceptual and Motor Skills, 72*, 40–42.

Tate, F. B., & Allen, H. (1985). Color preferences and the aged individual: Implications for art therapy. *Arts in Psychotherapy, 12*(3), 165–169.

Tobin, S. S., & Gustafson, J. D. (1987). What do we do differently with elderly clients? *Journal of Gerontological Social Work, 10*, 107–121.

Toepfer, C. T., Bicknell, A. T., & Shaw, D. O. (1974). Remotivation as behavior therapy. *Gerontologist, 14*, 451–453.

Tuttman, S. (1991). On utilizing humor in group psychotherapy. *Group, 15*, 246–256.

Viney, L. L., Benjamin, I. Y., & Preston, C. A. (1988). Promoting independence in the elderly: The role of psychological, social and physical constraints. *Clinical Gerontologist, 8*, 3–17.

Wald, J. (1986). Art therapy for patients with dementing illnesses. *Clinical Gerontologist, 4*, 29–40.

Wallace, J. B. (1992). Reconsidering the life review: The social construction of talk about the past. *The Gerontologist, 32*(1), 120–125.

Walter, J. L., & Peller, J. E. (1992). *Becoming solution-focused in brief therapy.* New York: Brunner/Mazel.

Waters, E. B., & Goodman, J. (1990). *Empowering older adults.* San Francisco: Jossey-Bass.

Watt, L. M., & Wong, P. (1991). A taxonomy of reminiscence and therapeutic implications. *Journal of Gerontological Social Work, 16*, 37–57.

Webster, J. D. & Haight, B. K. (1995). Memory lane milestones. In B. K. Haight & J. D. Webster (Eds.), *The art and science of reminiscing* (pp. 37–48). Washington, DC: Taylor & Francis.

Weiss, J. C. (1984). Expressive therapy with elders and the disabled. *Activities, Adaptation, and Aging, 5*(1–2), 213.

World Health Organization. (1992). *International statistical classification of diseases and related health problems* (ICD–10). Geneva, Switzerland: Author.

Yalom, I. D. (1985). *The theory and practice of group psychotherapy* (3rd ed.). New York: Basic Books.

Yalom, I. D., & Terrazas, F. (1968). Group therapy for psychotic elderly patients. *American Journal of Nursing, 68*(8), 1691–1694.

Yesavage, J. A., Brink, T. L., Lum, O., Huang, V., Adey, M., & Leirer, V. O. (1983). Development and validation of a geriatric depression screening scale: Preliminary report. *Psychiatric Research, 17*, 37–49.

Zimpfer, D. G. (1987). Groups for the aging; do they work? *Journal for Specialists in Group Work, 12*, 85–92.

Appendix A:
The GSE Model

INTRODUCTION TO GERIATRIC SKILLS ENHANCEMENT PROGRAM RATIONALE

Geriatric Skills Enhancement (GSE) is an interactive group program designed to address the skills deficits, social isolation, and significant losses of persons at various levels of functioning. GSE groups are directed at relearning, reinforcing, and practicing social skills for greater personal satisfaction and self-esteem.

Senior adults in a nursing home, assisted living facility, or within our communities become invisible people who must deal with one or more adjustments:

- current mobility limitations
- decreased income
- declining physical or mental capabilities
- frustrations of failing memory
- anger and agitation at life circumstances
- reduced social network due to illness, death, and relocation

Core Program Modules

Our groups are a series of rotating modules, including

Reminiscence	Bibliotherapy	Exploring Values and Roles
Music and Art	Phototherapy	Sensory Stimulation
Humor	Spirituality	Remotivation

Each group is conducted by a qualified group leader with a master's degree or doctoral training in counseling, psychology, or social work.

During GSE program modules, the primary group leader observes and carefully monitors the progress and participation of each group member. Our groups are limited to eight members to maximize the experience for each participant.

GSE program elements stimulate participants toward their highest potential ˊ level of functioning, socialization, and self-management.

GSE PROGRAM ENTRY

Senior adults are referred to GSE by their personal physicians, family, or facility staff. Each person is given a preliminary assessment to determine his or her level of functioning, brief social history, and suitability for group. The evaluation report is reviewed by the group leader and GSE program director to determine acceptance into the program. We welcome individuals who are willing to participate and have potential to benefit from our groups.

Entry Documentation

For each participant, we must have a copy of Medicare or Medicaid cards and Medigap Supplemental Insurance card, and the following must be read and signed by the participant or legal guardian, trustee, or health care surrogate.

- Financial Assignment and Release Form
- Statement of Participant Rights

Medicare/Insurance

GSE group services are covered by Medicare Part B and many supplemental insurance carriers. Any coverages apply toward service fees after the annual deductible has been met. Consult your coverage definitions for further information.

STATEMENT OF PARTICIPANT RIGHTS— GERIATRIC SKILLS ENHANCEMENT

We acknowledge the dignity and the rights of all participants and their families. Every effort is made to safeguard the legal and civil rights of participants who are voluntarily enrolled in GSE. Within 24 hours of acceptance into GSE or the next day that a GSE leader is at this location and before participating in your first group, you will be advised of these rights. You are given the opportunity to read this statement or request that it be read aloud to you. If your legal guardian, trustee, or health care surrogate cannot be present to review these rights at the same time you do, a copy will be provided to your representative in a timely manner.

1   Participants who are suitable for GSE groups as determined by testing and evaluation receive services without discrimination by race, religion, gender, ethnicity, age, or physical limitations.
2   Your civil rights and legal capacity are issues outside the scope of this program. GSE will accept the participant's status as determined by law along

with any legal restrictions imposed on the exercise of decisions for safety and welfare.
3 Every participant's personal dignity and privacy is recognized and respected in all GSE activities.
4 Each participant has different strengths and different needs that will be considered in an individualized treatment plan. In a skilled or assisted care facility, GSE's treatment plan will be integrated with the overall patient care plan. A review and update of this plan will occur regularly. The participant or guardian/trustee/health care surrogate may have input into this scheduled review.
5 The participant or guardian/trustee/health care surrogate receives program updates and notice of any significant changes on such matters as (a) group leader(s) and director responsible for GSE programs; (b) information on group modules and methods; (c) benefits or risks of participation in group; (d) right to refuse participation in research or training projects; (e) right to express complaint; (f) source of program reimbursement and any limitations on services imposed by third-party payers; (g) right to confidentiality of communication with group leader except under provisions of state law, including (1) approval given to submit claims information to third-party payers, (2) if there is reason to believe that you are a danger to yourself or others, (3) if you are a victim or perpetrator of child abuse or elder abuse; and (4) if a court order is given to disclose treatment information; and (h) right to obtain a copy of participant records or direct that the same be sent to another professional with a signed release of information.

In signing below, I read or heard the reading of this Statement of Participant Rights for GSE. My questions have been asked and answered. I now feel that I am ready and capable of signing this statement either for myself or acting in a legal capacity for the best interest of the participant.

Print Name of Participant _____

_____   _____
      Participant Signature   Date signed

OR

_____   _____
  Signature of Legal Representative   Date signed
Acting in capacity of: ❑ Guardian ❑ Trustee ❑ Health care Surrogate

_____   _____
   Witness to above signature   Date signed

_____   _____
  Accepted by GSE Representative   Date received

SUMMARY OF GSE BENEFITS TO FACILITY

A MEMO TO: Nursing Home
FROM: Geriatric Skills Enhancement
SUBJECT: Ten Ways GSE Groups Contribute to Your Facility

  1 We provide trained, qualified group leaders to conduct groups.

  2 We bring all program supplies used in core modules.

  3 Individualized treatment plans and ongoing evaluation are prepared for every group participant.

  4 We maintain documented progress notes for all participants.

  5 Our group leaders follow the medically accepted standards that govern charting in your notes, if this procedure is required.

  6 We accept full responsibility for billing to third-party payers.

  7 Continual review and updates of GSE modules and techniques occur to ensure program excellence.

  8 GSE leaders offer in-service training to help your staff understand our group concept and how it benefits participants.

  9 We are always willing to talk with participants' families or their representatives by personal or telephone appointment and with appropriate consent.

  10 We also enjoy talking with our participants and sharing the richness of their life experiences. A principal requirement for GSE group leaders is that they genuinely enjoy geriatric work and believe that elders have the right to socialization, personal growth, and unconditional respect regardless of age, physical limitation, or cognitive impairment.

COMMUNITY GROUP COVENANTS—GERIATRIC SKILLS ENHANCEMENT

I want to participant in the learning and fellowship of GSE groups at ABC Community Center and I agree to:

- attend regularly to get the most benefit from this experience
- respect the rights and opinions of all participants regardless of their gender, race, age, religion, ethnicity, or physical limitations
- keep information shared or heard within group confidential
- complete reading or other assignments given in group
- encourage others in their efforts to learn and share
- tell my group leader of any physical or emotional problems that might affect my participation or require any special assistance

I understand that if I break my commitment to confidentiality or behave in a disruptive or disrespectful manner, I will be asked to leave the group.

I am aware that this series of GSE groups are for education and personal growth only. These groups are not for counseling or psychotherapy, nor are they a substitute for psychological or medical treatment.

Print Name of Participant   _____

_____   _____
       Participant Signature   Date signed

_____   _____
  Accepted by GSE Representative   Date received

INTRODUCTION LETTER TO PHYSICIANS—
RE: NURSING HOME OR ASSISTED CARE PATIENTS

Offer this sample letter to the facility director to be sent on company letterhead:

Dear Doctor,

We are pleased to announce the addition of GERIATRIC SKILLS ENHANCEMENT to the fine services offered our residents. GSE is designed and customized for our needs by qualified group leaders with experience in working with the senior adult population.

A summary of GSE's overall program is enclosed. GSE Director, Psych O. Therapist, Ph.D., welcomes your questions about the suitability of these groups for your patients named below. Feel free to observe a GSE group on your next visit. GSE leaders are also licensed psychotherapists and social workers who are available for individual sessions with your patients on request.

Preentry evaluation begins March 1. Our nursing staff will call your office to receive the order to evaluate your patients.

Our patient care staff is enthusiastic about GSE. We support their goal to present innovative, interactive group modules that stimulate our patients to reach for and maintain their highest potential level of functioning, socialization, and self-esteem.

Sincerely,
Director, Nursing Home
Request evaluation orders for these patients:

_____

_____

_____

_____

TREATMENT PLAN/GERIATRIC SKILLS ENHANCEMENT

Name: _____   New Admit _____   Ongoing _____

Tx Plan Date _____

Psychosocial Test/Evaluation date: _____   Physical data _____   per chart _____

other diagnosis   _____   _____   _____

Problem 1: _____

Goal 1: _____

Problem 2: _____

Goal 2: _____

Treatment Plan reviewed by:

_____Therapist _____GSE Director

Review Date	OBJECTIVES: what patient does to meet goals	INTERVENTIONS: by Therapist to help patient meet goals	D O N E	P A R T I L	R E P E A T	T A R G E T

Appendix B:
List of Resources

Aesop's fables. (1989). New York: Barrons.

American Association of Music Therapy, P.O. Box 80012, Valley Forge, PA 19484; 610-265-4006.

American Association for Therapeutic Humor, 1441 Shermer Ave., Suite 110, Northbrook, IL 60062.

Analects of Confucius (Arthur Waley, Trans.). (1938). New York: Random House.

Annual Register of Grant Support: A Directory of Funding Sources. New York: R. R. Bowker.

Birren, F. (1992). *Color psychology and color therapy.* (Rev. ed.). Secaucus, NY: Carol Publishing

Comedy Cart, Morton Plant Mease Hospital, 323 Jeffords St., Clearwater, FL 34617; 813-462-7000.

Cousins, N. (1979). *Anatomy of an illness.* New York: W. W. Norton.

Directory of Biomedical and Healthcare Grants. Phoenix, AZ: Oryx Press.

Eldersong Newsletter (B. Karras, Ed). Mount Airy, MD: Eldersong Publications, Inc.; 301-829-0533. $15 per year or $26 for 2 years.

Forer, L. (1976). *The birth order factor: How your personality is influenced by your place in the family.* New York: McKay Co.

Frost, R. (1969). The road not taken. In E. C. Lathem (Ed.), *The poetry of Robert Frost* (p. 105). New York: Holt, Rinehart & Winston.

Funny bones don't get arthritis: Humor for the young at heart (#P109). Mt. Airy, MD: Eldersong Publications, Inc.; 301-829-0533.

Goodman, J. The Humor Project, 110 Spring Street, Saratoga Springs, NY 12866. Quarterly publication and resource lists.

Homer. (1919). *The Odyssey* (A. T. Murray, Trans.). London: W. Heinemann.

Isaacson, C. E. (1988). *Understanding yourself through birth order.* Algona, IA: Upper Des Moines Counseling Center.

Jensen, M. D. (1991). *Old is older than me.* San Bernardino, CA: Here's Life Publishers.

Journal of Poetry Therapy.

Khayyam, O. (1906). *Rubaiyat in the quatrains of Omar Hayyam of Nishapur* (Eben Francis, Trans.). Worchester, MA: Commonwealth Press.

Leonard, F. (1987). *Read aloud programs or elderly project: An instructional manual.* Seattle, WA: Seattle Public Library.

Life guidance through literature. (1992). Chicago: American Library Association.

Linkletter, A. (1957). *Kids say the darndest things.* Englewood Cliffs, NJ: Prentice Hall.

McGoldrick, M., & Gerso, R. (1985). *Genograms in family assessment.* New York: W. W. Norton.

Modern Maturity. Magazine of the American Association of Retired People (AARP).

Mother Goose rhymes. (1980). New York: Golden Press. (Original published 1760 as *Mother Goose's melody)*

Myers, J. E. (1992). *A treasury of senior adult humor.* Springfield, IL: Lincoln-Herndon Press.

National Association for Music Therapy, 8455 Colesville Road, Suite 930, Silver Spring, MD 20910; 301-589-3300.

National Institutes of Health, Bethesda, MD (includes National Institute on Mental Health and National Institute on Aging); 301-496-4000.

National Remotivation Therapy Technique Organization, 1400 Roosevelt Blvd, Philadelphia, PA 19114; 215-671-4939. Information and training.

NatureQuest—An adventure in nature and music (cassette tapes with classical and original music that complements sounds of forest, ocean, rain, birds, and other outdoor experiences). North Word Press, Inc., P.O. Box 1360, Minocqua, WI 54548. Available at some music and discount stores.

Orwell, G. (1961). *1984.* New York: New American Library.

Pardeck, J. T. (1993). *Using bibliotherapy in clinical practice: A guide to self help books.* Westport, CT: Greenwood Press.

Poe, E. A. The raven. In *Complete stories and poems of Edgar Allan Poe* (p. 754). Garden City, NY: Doubleday Co.

Radeloff, D. J. (1990). Role of color in perception of attractiveness. *Perceptual and Motor Skills, 71,* 151–160.

Reader's digest. Pleasantville, NY 10570.

Reminisce (magazine). Reiman Publications, P.O. Box 998, Greendale, WI 53129.

Remotivation kits. American Psychiatric Association, 1700 8th St. NW, Washington, DC 20009; 202-682-6000.

Research centers directory. Detroit, MI: Gale Research.

Sharpe, D. T. (1974). *The psychology of color and design.* Chicago: Nelson-Hall Co.

Tagore, R. (1928/1966). *Fireflies.* New York: The Macmillan Company.

Tommy Thumb's pretty song book. (Original published 1744)

Verne, J. (1931). From the Earth to the moon. *The omnibus Jules Verne.* Philadelphia: Lippincott. Available in inexpensive paperback reprints in discount book stores and in the children's section of book stores.

Verne, J. (1931). Twenty thousand leagues under the sea. *The omnibus Jules Verne.* Philadelphia: Lippincott. Available in inexpensive paperback reprints in discount book stores and in the children's section of book stores.

Videos related to remotivation topics, including transportation modes, baseball legends, American nostalgia, and view of the ocean. Eldersong Publications, Inc., P.O. Box 74, Mt. Airy, MD 21771; 301-829-0533.

Whitman, W. (1940). *Leaves of grass.* New York: Doubleday, Doran.

Index